"*Entreat me not to leave thee, and to return from following after thee; for whither thou goest, I will go; and where thou lodgest, I will lodge; thy people shall be my people; and thy God my God.*"

—Ruth (to Naomi)

"*The Master is here, and calleth for thee*" (K. J. V.).

—Martha (to Mary)

"*Go . . . . tell . . . . .*"

—The Risen Christ
(to Mary of Magdala)

WOMEN
OF SCRIPTURE

BY

ARTHUR BRUCE MOSS

Minister of
John Street Methodist Church
New York City

Woman's Division of Christian Service
Board of Missions and Church Extension
The Methodist Church

ARTHUR BRUCE MOSS was born in New York City. His parents, Frank Moss and Eva Estelle Bruce, were active as young people in the old Thirty-seventh Street Methodist Church, and later in Trinity and St. James Methodist churches in Harlem.

Mr. Moss attended the public schools of New York City. He received the degree of bachelor of arts from Columbia University and bachelor of divinity from Drew Theological Seminary. He was awarded a fellowship for a year of graduate study at the United Free Church College, Glasgow, Scotland, in the department of New Testament under the late Professor James Denney. Further work at Drew and a residence and research seminar in the lands of the Bible led to the degree of master of arts.

After returning from Glasgow, he served brief periods as pastor at the Metropolitan Temple and at Woodycrest Methodist Church, in New York. This service was followed by three years of intensive work in India for the Board of Foreign Missions just prior to the Centenary Movement, and for a number of years Mr. Moss was the associate secretary for India on the staff of this board.

Since 1926 he has served three pastorates in the New York East Conference: Jamaica (Queens), New York Avenue (Brooklyn), Bay Shore (Long Island); and is now at historic John Street Church, in lower Manhattan, the oldest Methodist church in America.

To the Memory of my Mother
EVA BRUCE MOSS
whose utterly unselfish life,
devout prayer experience, and
unremitting devotion to her
home and to her church
have ever been a guiding star.

FOREWORD

The Bible—Word of God

The Bible has many widely differing elements, each fascinating in its own right. Here we find all we may ever know in exact record of the Saviour's life, his deeds of love and merciful power, the way he lived among people, his incomparable words. Back of him is the record of God's dealing with the Hebrew people, astonishingly full and accurate in detail when we consider the problems of primitive writing, copying, and preservation of documents. There are impassioned public utterances, noble and exalted poetry—both lyric and epic—historical records in prose, exquisitely fashioned epigrams, drama, fiction, avowed fables, hymns, personal letters, a whole literature of prayer and devotion.

All these conspire together to form the vehicle of expression for the eternal and living Word of God. This is the ageless truth and immeasurable love of God so simply told that he who runs may read, and yet so profound that it carries in its mighty cadences the salvation of the world.

> The earth shall be full of the knowledge of Jehovah, as the waters cover the sea.[1]
>
> God was in Christ reconciling the world unto himself.[2]

Beyond the power of any merely human mind to state, richer than the capacity of any human heart to imagine, abides this Word of God. Thus we know the Book to be inspired—literally "breathed within"—of the Holy Spirit.

[1]Isa. 11:9.
[2]Cor. 5:19.

With the wonder of its divine inspiration, the Bible is, nevertheless, essentially human in character. The authors of its various books are individuals quite like ourselves. Kings and fishermen contributed to its pages. Men of wealth and high position as well as those of humble circumstance, some professionally educated and others who never enjoyed formal schooling, stand side by side in its composition. All save one were Hebrews. Yet that Gentile, Luke the physician, made one of the largest personal contributions of the many writers.[1]

They lived vividly as men, and with relentless candor they revealed their own shortcomings and failures equally with their joys and triumphs. Without fear or favor and with a frankness and truth seldom equaled, they told the thrilling stories of their heroes and heroines, as well as of their villains. The unquenched hopes of the human spirit, and the unceasing love and abiding truth of God were always uppermost in their writing. Despite the distances of time and space that separate us from those who wrote the Bible, we find them ever dealing with the timeless verities of human nature. The Book is thus the constant contemporary of all ages and all peoples.

Imperishable portraits are painted before our eyes as we read the Bible. Brave men who dared, and fell, and rose again, and triumphed, walk there, etched against the background of their day. Women who loved, and struggled, and served, making life so much the better because they had lived, stand erect beside their men. Children, in adorable infancy and joyous growth, move across the pages with mingled tears and laughter, as is their wont. And ever in their words and deeds we glimpse the beauty and the light,

---

[1]He wrote Luke and Acts, which should always be read and thought of as the two volumes of a single major work.

the blessed grace and power, the eternal, vital meaning of the love of God.

Acknowledgments and Notes

The Scripture quotations in this book are from the American Standard Version of the Revised Bible, copyright, 1929, by the International Council of Religious Education, and used by permission.

Appreciation is expressed to Charles Scribner's Sons for their kind permission to include certain quotations from *Personalities of the Old Testament*, by Fleming James, and to Harper and Brothers for similar permission to quote from *Encyclopedia of Bible Life*, by M. S. and J. L. Miller, and to Madeleine Sweeney Miller, who has graciously permitted quotation of her poem, "To Martha at Bethany: Spring 33 A.D."

Suggestions are offered to those who project serious Bible study, whether as individuals or as a group. Use both the American Standard Version and the King James Version. Other specialized translations will be found helpful at many points. If facility is had in language other than English, by all means read in that language also. Frequently passages that may seem obscure or capable of diverse interpretation are clarified by the idiom or vocabulary of another language that is not open to ambiguity. Carefully check all marginal notes and references in the biblical texts that are used. Make complete written notes.

The following helps are recommended:

A Concordance of the Bible

A Bible dictionary

Probably the best one-volume commentary on the entire

Bible is *The Abingdon Bible Commentary*.* For purposes of reference in this study, this volume is identified as ABC in footnotes.

Immeasurably valuable is *Encyclopedia of Bible Life*, by M. S. and J. L. Miller. The illustrations alone are worth the cost of the volume. In the footnotes of this study the symbol EBL is used in reference to this work.

A visit to the public library will reveal a wealth of standard aids and cognate material.

---

*All books referred to in this text may be ordered from The Methodist Publishing House.

Women of Scripture

The home in its greatly varied activities and interests claimed the enterprise and energy of practically every woman mentioned in the Bible. Some were wives and mothers, giving glad affection to their children, their constant thought to the needs of the household. Others were childless through the lengthening years, facing ever the severe problems of readjustment which the social usages of the day forced upon them. Queens and slaves, socially as far asunder as the poles, proved of equal consequence before God in the light of life's intense demands. The saddened widow with the heavy economic problem, and the woman of wealth glad to serve the Lord she loved, together with the outlander of an alien race, and the one forced to flee under religious persecution, older sister of our modern displaced persons, touched hands over the centuries. And all were women of the household, great or small, as the home stood at the common center of their hearts' devotion.

The personality, life and work of certain women of the Scriptures, constitutes the theme of this study. We shall, then, visit first their homes, eager to sense the meaning life held for them, to touch with reverence for a moment the fabric of love they wove. Yet, of compelling necessity, the home ever moves out in widening circles of radiating contact with others. It does so with us, today. It did with them, then. We shall walk some of their roads of broader relationship as these older women ventured upon them. Women of our day have journeyed far into these specialized fields, have entered deeply into the vast complexities of modern life. We may be startled to discover how far some women of the Bible traveled in these directions. Indeed, their experiences may aid us in finer solution of the problems we face. Primarily, they were ever aware of God. This sense of his continuing nearness was companionship and comfort to many of them. This experience must be ours also, even in what seems to us the completely modern landscape of this age-old road of life.

In pursuing this study we shall, of course, draw upon the wealth of knowledge available to us in the work of scholars who have studied the history and customs of the biblical peoples. Our chief source-book, however, will be the Bible itself. The words and deeds of these notable women are recorded on its pages. Its records provide the immediate setting and background of their lives and personalities. Thus the Bible will ever be at the heart of our work. It is a vital and living book, replete with the love and service and sacrifice of people like ourselves. The writer eagerly hopes that many friends will be inspired to further, habitual study of the Bible itself, prompted by a new interest in the women who move across its pages. This deepened interest in the Bible is the ultimate goal of our study together.

CONTENTS

Chapter One

Nurture and Training in the Home

INFLUENCE OF THE HOME

THE BELIEFS and the practices of religion are astonishingly potent in the realms of daily conduct and human relationship. The true test of character lies in the profound moral and spiritual convictions of the soul. These are conveyed more powerfully through religious faith and its tenets, and through the forms of worship natural to the believer, than by any other force that affects the spirit. A person's concepts of God, of other men, of the world about him, and of his privileges and duties involved therein are the norms whereby his standards of value and action are formed. Present these standards to a person and obtain his acceptance of them and devotion to them, and one has largely determined his character and the general course of action of his life. Occasionally "the unpredictability of human conduct" is startlingly demonstrated in a court of law, on the field of battle, or under the onslaught of fierce temptation. Because of what may appear to be the unexpected reversal of character, the event is deeply moving. Careful note should be made of the fact that this "unpredictability" in any given case is almost always due to our ignorance of the actual standards of value held by the individual prior to the dramatic incident.

1

There are these ancient and timeless words:

> For as he thinketh within himself, so is he.[1]

> Whatsoever things are true, whatsoever things are honorable, whatsoever things are just, whatsoever things are pure, whatsoever things are lovely, whatsoever things are of good report; if there be any virtue, and if there be any praise, think on these things.[2]

> Let the words of my mouth and the meditation of my heart be acceptable in thy sight, O Jehovah, my rock, and my redeemer.[3]

RELIGION IN THE HOME

In literally countless instances the superb success or the sad failure of men and women may be directly traceable to the presence or absence of vital religion in the childhood home. There is something stimulating beyond all words to describe in the living validity of mother's prayers and father's faith. By their precious memory and abiding power many a man is sustained against terrific pressures, many a woman is steadied in the twisting circumstances that are peculiarly her own. A meaningless vacuum is so often left in the soul when no such holy memory abides. The test comes—and no instinctive light shines in the darkness, no treasured words of human trust and divine love echo in a voice revered.

The home that is supremely blest enshrines religious devotion, faith, and practice in the hour of its joyous establishment. In mutual trust, glorified by faith in God and devout worship, husband and wife enter its portals side by side. Equally is this true for the many single persons, men and women, who make their dwelling a center of sacred influence and glorious spiritual life. With the ineffable divine radiance and the holy standards affirmed, the room, apartment, or the house if it be so, becomes truly a home. And God is there, and life is good.

---

[1]Prov. 23:7.   [2]Phil. 4:8.   [3]Ps. 19:14.

2

The Faith of Children

A baby is a genuine person from his birth. The initial test of obedience and the definite assertion of his own will and desires, come before the child is many weeks old. The joys of possession, and of the use of his own things, evidence themselves almost before the parents realize their effective presence. Habits of action, the estimate of values, emotion, and a sense of right and wrong are his before the first words are lisped or the stumbling step is taken. The rich ground of personality is already thickly sown with seed—some fine grain, some tares—and the tiny sprouts of fruitage will appear ere the first two years are past.[1]

The growing child's awareness of the meaning of mother's words and deeds is amazingly greater than his stammering speech or fumbling imitation would seem to indicate. The name of God and of the Saviour, the posture of prayer, lovely little melodies, simple bits of sacred verse, may be inculcated very early, if the devout parents will take the time and make the careful effort. Truth in utterance, obedience in action, honesty in thought, fairness in play, tenderness in contact, bravery in the face of temptation, loving service, sacrifice for others, may be readily learned, and absorbed by the soul. The harder disciplines utterly necessary for righteous living will not be easy subjects, but their glad pursuit and attainment are priceless.

Training by precept will advance until the Book itself lies open to the child. Every advantage of material should be utilized, and there is a wealth of it ready to our hands. The trained teaching personnel of the church school and the association there with other children in corporate learning,

---

[1]Read again carefully the Saviour's parables of the Sower, the Tares, the Harvest. Consider them in primary relation to the religious training of the children you dearly love.

3

worship, and service will greatly help by supplementing the resources of the home. But wise are the parents who make it their own joyous responsibility to be the major elements in guiding and stimulating their children's moral and spiritual growth. Profoundly rich are the precepts when they seem but the natural and glorious expression of the full and beautiful life of the home itself. The truest teaching and the noblest precepts, however carefully given, may be completely negated by the word or deed of parents, or by the careless indifference of the home.

SARAH, WIFE OF ABRAHAM

Sarah is the earliest truly vital person to be found among the women of Scripture. Character and personality come alive with her. The women noted as having lived before her day are but vague and shadowy at best. She is the first to possess enough historic authenticity and definite individuality to permit full portraiture in the astonishing gallery of the women of the Bible.

As the wife of Abraham, Sarah journeyed with him when his father, Terah, left Ur in the far south of Mesopotamia.[1] They tarried first in the vicinity of Haran, where Terah died. As the oldest son, Abraham then became head of the entire household or clan. Soon afterwards Abraham and Sarah resumed the long journey, curving southwestward into the land of Canaan, which was later to be known as Palestine.[2] The total journey can be estimated at about a

[1]Scholars date the migration at about 1800 B.C., allowing a possible century either way (see ABC, pp. 61, 108). The record of Abraham's life and wanderings is found in Genesis 11:10 through 25:18. These chapters should be read carefully as a whole, for they are basic to the history and growth of the Hebrew people and of their religion, and to a large area of Christianity as well.
[2]Gen. 12:1-9.

4

thousand miles. Considering the distance, the number of people involved and the extent of their flocks and herds, the hazards in changing terrain, scanty food and water supply, and the menace of brigands, one realizes that this was a migration requiring marked ability for organization and an effective power of leadership in the patriarch. Terah began the enterprise at Ur, and Abraham brought it to completion from Haran to Canaan.[1]

Sarah was unusually beautiful of countenance,[2] endowed with a winsome and attractive personality. Indeed, on two occasions a king was enamored of her to such a degree that he desired her for his harem,[3] causing much embarrassment until her status as Abraham's wife was clearly indicated.[4] She evidently possessed a quick and alert mind, and an eager readiness to follow with Abraham in the broadly changing circumstances of their migratory life.

The incidents connected with the apparently cruel banishing of Hagar, Sarah's Egyptian handmaid, and her young son, Ishmael, constitute what has often been thought of as a serious blot upon Sarah's character.[5] Her original proffer of Hagar to Abraham as a secondary wife, and the subsequent birth of Ishmael, was in strict accord with the highest social ethics of their day, and was intended to preserve the noblest sanctities they knew. It is true that the resultant situation was filled with angry passion and harsh deeds. Nevertheless, it is hardly fair for us to judge Abraham, Sarah, and Hagar in this delicate relationship by

---

[1]The vivid story of Abraham's rescue of Lot from the eastern marauders (Gen. 14) is indicative of his strength. The probability of Amraphel of the scriptural account being the historic Hammurabi of Babylon would rather definitely fix the dates for Abraham's life.

[2]Gen. 12:11, 14.

[3]Gen. 12:10 ff., and chapter 20.

[4]She was Abraham's half-sister as well as his wife (Gen. 20:12).

[5]Gen. 16:1-16; 21:8-21.

5

Christian ethical standards of which they had never dreamed. Neither should it be forgotten that when Abraham died, "Isaac and Ishmael his sons buried him in the cave of Machpelah,"[1] as though no radical differences had ever existed between them.

Sarah, Stay to Abraham in Answering God's Call

In words that have been treasured by every succeeding generation, God had spoken to Abraham:

> Get thee out of thy country, and from thy kindred, and from thy father's house, unto the land that I will show thee: and I will make of thee a great nation, and I will bless thee, and make thy name great; and be thou a blessing: and I will bless them that bless thee, and him that curseth thee will I curse: and in thee shall all the families of the earth be blessed.[2]

To this amazing call of Jehovah, Abraham, who up till then had doubtless been a worshiper of the moon god of Ur, gave complete allegiance and instant obedience. This was the compelling reason for his leaving Haran for Canaan. With him loyally toiled Sarah, equal with him in the new faith, side by side with him in dutiful obedience. There is no shadow of doubt but that her sustaining devotion and unquestioning confidence were mighty factors in Abraham's loyalty to God's startling command.

Soon there came another step in their companionship with God, as he spoke further to Abraham:

> . . . . Fear not, Abram: I am thy shield, and thy exceeding great reward . . . . . Look now toward heaven, and number the stars, if thou be able to number them: . . . . So shall thy seed be. And he believed in Jehovah; and he reckoned it to him for righteousness.[3]

---

[1] Gen. 25:9. "The generations of Ishmael" are formally recorded in Gen. 25:12-16, before the generations of Isaac, as evidence of Ishmael's being older than Isaac.

[2] Gen. 12:1-3.

[3] Gen. 15:1, 5, 6. From this theme Paul, in Romans 4, develops a telling argument for the Christian conception of the interrelation of faith and righteousness.

On still a later day Jehovah spoke again to Abraham, sealing the original command and promise with the terms of a definite covenant equally binding upon himself and Abraham:

> I am God Almighty[1]; walk before me, and be thou perfect. And I will make my covenant between me and thee, and will multiply thee exceedingly.[2]

Abraham and Sarah gave prompt and explicit obedience to the terms of the new covenant with God, and accepted the incredible promise of a son of their own union, even in the face of their advanced years.[3]

Isaac, Son of Abraham and Sarah

The third and supreme test of Abraham's faith lay in his acceptance of and immediate obedience to God's strange command that he offer Isaac as a sacrifice of devotion.[4] At the moment of crisis his hand was stayed by the divine voice:

> Lay not thy hand upon the lad, neither do thou anything unto him; for now I know that thou fearest God, seeing thou hast not withheld thy son, thine only son, from me . . . . because thou hast done this thing, ... in thy seed shall all the nations of the earth be blessed; because thou hast obeyed my voice.[5]

The rearing and training of Isaac, born to Sarah late in life, presented unusual problems, but they were surmounted by her natural grace and application. This duty rested with the women of the household, and in such a situation as Sarah faced, she would take a large share of that responsibility personally. The limitation of material at her disposal for his nurture in daily conduct and religious faith is start-

---

[1]The Hebrew is *El Shaddai*, a name for God not previously given.

[2]Gen. 17:1, 2. The entire chapter should be read in this connection.

[3]So great was their joy and faith that they both instinctively laughed aloud. When the son came in due time, he was called Isaac, which means "laughter."

[4]Gen. 22:1-19.

[5]Gen. 22:12, 16, 18.

7

ling when we think about it. There were no Ten Commandments to be set up as standards for his life—centuries were still to elapse ere Moses would proclaim them to the awed and waiting people at the foot of Sinai.[1] No lovely and tender Psalms were ready, with David's sweet melody for lullaby—a thousand years must pass before the shepherd king would give them voice. The hope of a Redeemer was yet to burgeon[2]—it only lay like a seed just sown in God's promise, "in thee shall all the families of the earth be blessed." Working with what she had of tribal tradition and custom, purged and ennobled by the new flame of devotion to Jehovah, she sedulously gave Isaac her very soul's life. He grew to be a noble follower of the God of his father and mother, with loyal love and devotion to them both. The highest honor Isaac could pay to Sarah was to treasure her own tent, unoccupied from the day of her passing, until he could offer it to Rebekah when she came to be his wife. Only then "Isaac was comforted after his mother's death."[3]

The Character of Sarah

Through the lengthened years and across the uncounted miles, Sarah had known no other home but that tent of heavy black material woven from goat's hair.[4] After leaving Ur as a young wife, she never lived in a house. With her husband she was a constant migrant. There were numerous servants to fetch and carry, it is true. There was wealth of the sort for which men like Abraham might care. But there was continuous privation—a minimum of the delicate things of life—the jolting back of a camel on long journeys, a rug thrown over the hard-packed sand of the

[1]Exod. 19:16—20:21.
[2]Isa. 52, 53.
[3]Gen. 24:67.
[4]EBL, pp. 238-240, see the important section on Tent-Homes.

desert for a couch. With Abraham, her husband, she was loyal and faithful to Jehovah, and she made ceaseless contribution to his companionship with God by her own uncomplaining and understanding fidelity.[1]

Sarah demonstrated gifts of leadership blent with rare ability to follow and to sacrifice. By these powers and her charming personality, she kept the enduring fidelity and devotion of Abraham, and gave to him the vitality of her own faith.

THE INFLUENCE OF THREE WOMEN UPON THE LIFE OF MOSES

Jochebed, Mother of Leaders

Amram and his wife, Jochebed,[2] both of the tribe of Levi, lived in a mud house close to one of the many canals in the eastern section of the Nile River delta. For several generations their forebears had toiled there as slaves of Egypt— ever since "there arose a new king [dynasty] over Egypt, who knew not Joseph."[3] The most arduous types of manual labor had been their lot:

> And the Egyptians made the children of Israel to serve with rigor: and they made their lives bitter with hard service, in mortar and in brick, and in all manner of service in the field, all their service, wherein they made them serve with rigor.[4]

These slaved, with the many others of their kind, in what seemed a futureless serfdom. Year after year, generation upon generation, for fully three centuries, the sons of

---

[1]Isaiah records God's words to him as "Abraham my friend"—41:8; and James, the brother of the Lord, refers to this, saying: "he was called the friend of God"—2:23.

[2]Exod. 6:20; Num. 26:59.

[3]Exod. 1:8.

[4]Exod. 1:13, 14. This service doubtless included construction of dykes and canals to control and distribute the Nile waters, as well as heavy agricultural work.

9

Jacob had suffered. No change could ever come, or so it seemed, and the exactions and repressive laws against them grew ever more severe.

Into the home of Amram and Jochebed came a daughter, Miriam, and then a son, Aaron. Soon after the birth of the son, the most brutally repressive edict was issued by the Pharaoh.[1] This rescript ordered the killing of all Hebrew male babies at birth.[2] When Miriam was possibly ten years of age, another baby was born to Jochebed. She had seen the misery of many other mothers when their newborn baby boys had perished under Rameses' inhuman edict. Surely she must contrive somehow to save this precious baby's life. She managed to hide him for three months, but this became increasingly difficult as he grew. Then a way seemed to open.

Daughter of Pharaoh, Foster Mother of Moses

Miriam had noted that the Princess Merris, daughter of Pharaoh Rameses, frequently walked with her ladies along the bank of the royal canal in the cool of the day. So Jochebed and Miriam made their plan. The edict had required that the infants be thrown into the river. This they would indeed do, but in a most unusual way. "In a small, mud-daubed boat of papyrus, miniature of the large papyrus boats in which rich Egyptian families went hunting in their marshes, the infant Moses was hidden amid the camouflage of Nile reeds."[3] Miriam hovered near, keeping watch. Soon the royal party approached.[4] The princess herself spied the craft, and it was brought to her. Alone,

[1]Probably Rameses II, c. 1290-1225 B.C. (see notes in ABC *ad loc*).
[2]Exod. 1:15-22.
[3]EBL, p. 214.
[4]Exod. 2:5-9.

10

and surrounded by these strangers, the baby cried. His wail went to Merris' heart, and she claimed him for her own.[1] Miriam, who had quietly drawn near, astutely arranged for Jochebed to become the baby's nurse on Merris' behalf.

Thus Jochebed's baby was saved from the fate of many another Hebrew infant, and for the amazing destiny that was to be his, under God. As a growing lad he passed from his home to the royal palace, there to receive such education as befitted the adopted son of the princess. Merris gave him his name, which we call "Moses." It was a common Egyptian name for a boy, meaning "man," or "son."[2] The arts of government were instilled in his eager mind, together with those wider ranges of knowledge open to Egypt's chosen. Yet, deeper than all else, there lived in his heart the traditions and hopes of his enslaved people,[3] their folklore and their songs as he had learned them from Jochebed and Miriam. And he treasured a rich and enduring love for his sister, who had so effectively helped to save his life at his birth, and who was destined to play no small part in the progress of his own great career.[4]

During the brief years that Jochebed had Moses at her side, she apparently trained him with the utmost care. So devout and earnest was his faith in the God of his fathers that he remained true to him in face of the sumptuous and attractive idolatry he witnessed in the pageantry of Egypt's royal worship. The compelling demands of right conduct had struck deep into his nature. So profound was

---

[1]Further discussion of this incident occurs in the chapter "Across the Boundaries of Race," pp. 80-82.

[2]Exod. 2:10. It is found in her father's name, "Ra-meses," which means "son (worshiper) of Ra."

[3]Exod. 2:11-25.

[4]Miriam's work is discussed in the chapter "Career and Business Women," pp. 55-59.

11

this influence that he was chosen of God to receive on Sinai that epitome of righteous living that we call the Ten Commandments. His moral perception was equal to receiving and transmitting this test and standard in so simple a form that it continues valid for all time.

Miriam, Sister of Moses

Jochebed had Miriam and Aaron at home with her many years longer than she had Moses. His towering personality looms so great against the horizon of his day that we tend to forget his sister and brother. But they, also, were trained with unremitting care. Miriam evidenced definite talents of leadership. She did not marry. Yet, despite the fact of such unusual social status, she apparently assumed a post of religious prestige among the women of her group. Aaron did not possess powers duplicating those of Moses. But he had the ability of faithfully following a leader, and of carrying out the details of a given plan of work. He also was blest with a readiness of speech.[1] His fluency of utterance was equal in the language of the Egyptian court and in the vernacular of the Hebrews. With her youngest child adopted as son of a princess of the ruling house, did Jochebed have an unvoiced intuition that he might, on a day, free his people, and in that freedom lay broad the foundations of God's kingdom? Did she ever dream that Miriam and Aaron might aid Moses in such a triumph as only devoted and talented sister and brother could do? In the ultimate of things this actually occurred. Moses would have been sore put to it had not Aaron been with him as his very voice and his loyal active agent. Miriam's command over the women was a great asset. We owe Jochebed a debt of honor

---

[1]Exod. 4:10-17; 6:28—7:1.

we gladly pay. Her children, true to her teaching, live in the vital faith we hold today.

HANNAH, MOTHER OF SAMUEL

The story of the birth of Samuel and of his consecration to Jehovah is one of the most beautiful in the entire sweep of Scripture.[1] Indeed, it is the classic instance in the Old Testament of the worth of zealous religious training in early childhood.

A century had elapsed since Deborah and Barak gave freedom to the northern Hebrew tribes by breaking the power of Jabin, last of the Canaanite kings. This had been achieved in a terrific battle in a driving storm along the banks of the swollen Kishon River.[2] Gideon and others had offered the land a measure of protection against raiders from east of the Jordan.[3] The marauding Philistines had suffered a temporary setback in the hardy exploits of Samson. By the time of Samuel, however, they were again on the rampage in great strength. They were actually to capture the sacred ark at Ebenezer,[4] and there adminster to the Hebrews so disastrous a defeat as would hold them in subservience until the rise of David as king, after Saul's death.

From the days of Joshua and Deborah, no "judge" had given the people any really constructive spiritual leadership. They had all been men of war and fierce battle. None were of the type who could promote moral and religious advance. It is true that the ark had been located at Beth-el,[5]

---

[1] I Sam. 1 through 3.
[2] The significance of Deborah and her work is discussed in the chapter on "Career and Business Women," pp. 60-65.
[3] Judg. 6 ff.
[4] I Sam. 4:2-22.
[5] Judg. 20:26, 27.

and then in a permanent shrine at Shiloh.[1] Numbers of the Hebrews made regular pilgrimage there to pay their devotions. Priestly families appear to have held the holy place, the last representatives being the mild Eli and his wicked sons. Doubtless many of the people worshiped Jehovah in sincere piety, and, to the best of their ability, followed the customs and ethical teachings of Moses. But no dynamic spiritual leader stood before them as a guide, and without such a "judge" the loss of the ark from Shiloh, soon to be experienced, might well have been fatal to the faith and cult of Jehovah. "The need of the hour was for some man of God who could arouse new and prodigious forces in the depressed people and put the whole national life on a higher level. The story of Samuel[2] tells how in the providence of God that need was supplied."[3]

Her Prayer for a Son

Close relationship with Eli, priest of the ark at Shiloh, was evidently enjoyed by Elkanah who dwelt at Ramah, in the hill country of Ephraim some distance north of Jerusalem.[4] This man had two wives, Peninnah who reared him a family, and Hannah whom he loved devotedly but who was childless. For a long time she had prayed in great earnestness for a son to crown their love, but no child had come. Finally, on a year when they were at Shiloh for the sacrifice, she went into the temple of the ark to the most sacred spot to which she might have access:

[1] I Sam. 3:3.

[2] I Sam. 1 through 19; also 25:1.

[3] Fleming James, *Personalities of the Old Testament* (New York: Charles Scribner's Sons, 1947), p. 77.

[4] I Sam. 1. The complete name of the place was Ramathaim-zophim (1:1). It may have been the ancient site of the Arimathea of Jesus' day from which had come the councilor, Joseph, who gave his new tomb for the Saviour's burial (Matt. 27:57-60).

> And she was in bitterness of soul, and prayed unto Jehovah, and wept sore. And she vowed a vow, and said, O Jehovah of hosts, if thou wilt indeed look on the affliction of thy handmaid, and remember me, and not forget thy handmaid, but wilt give unto thy handmaid a man-child, then I will give him unto Jehovah all the days of his life, and there shall no razor come upon his head.[1]

Eli the priest, at his accustomed place in the shrine, noted the intensity of Hannah's devotion. After talking with her about the problem, he gave her this blessing:

> Go in peace; and the God of Israel grant thy petition that thou hast asked of him.[2]

With new joy, the like of which she had not known for many days, Hannah returned to Ramah with her husband. In process of time she bore Elkanah a son, "and she called his name Samuel, saying, Because I have asked him of Jehovah."[3]

Her Dedication of Samuel

Hannah kept Samuel close with her at Ramah until he came to boyhood. Then, when he was old enough to understand, she and Elkanah took him to Shiloh. With formal prayers and sacrificial ceremony, they presented him to Eli for consecration to Jehovah and for constant service at the shrine. Hannah's noble words will ever be treasured:

> For this child I prayed; and Jehovah hath given me my petition which I asked of him: therefore also I have granted him to Jehovah; as long as he liveth he is granted to Jehovah.[4]

Samuel apparently was six or seven years of age when he was thus dedicated to a lifetime of priestly service before Jehovah. Within a short space the boy had proven himself so pure in heart and so worthy of his parents' consecration that he was privileged to wear the holy vestment of the

[1] I Sam. 1:10, 11.
[2] I Sam. 1:17.
[3] I Sam. 1:20.
[4] I Sam. 1:27, 28.

15

ephod in his daily ministry before the ark of Jehovah and at the altar with the people.

> But Samuel ministered before Jehovah, being a child, girded with a linen ephod. Moreover his mother made him a little robe, and brought it to him from year to year, when she came up with her husband to offer the yearly sacrifice.[1]

Ramah was not very far from Shiloh, and there were doubtless other frequent contacts between the young priest and his home. Yet, the fact that Hannah made his sacred vestments with her own hands, renewing and fitting them as he grew from year to year, deepened most profoundly in his heart the meaning of his mother's faith. She was thus very intimately related to his personal devotional life and to his public priestly office before Jehovah on behalf of the worshiping people.

Her Gifts to Samuel

Hannah had given Samuel the spiritual insight her own soul possessed. In eager hope her prayers enfolded him from the moment of Eli's blessing at Shiloh. The sanctity of the Law of Moses as held in a Levite home, the fact of his dedication to Jehovah from before his birth, the tender love of such a mother as was Hannah, his acceptance as a tiny child of these holy influences—such were the factors that brought the seeds of his own rich personality to early growth, lovely flower, and priceless harvest.

Samuel was Samuel, it is true, just as every individual stands inviolate in the right of his own free personality. The spiritual growth of the lad from Ramah was such that he became the first outstanding national priest among the Hebrews, the author of the constitution of their theocratic

---

[1] I Sam. 2:18, 19. Read carefully Exodus 28 where the beautiful pattern of the ephod and the robe worn under it is given and their symbolism indicated.

16

monarchy, the leader qualified to choose and anoint both Saul and David as king, as well as the founder of the noble order of the true prophets of Jehovah. He is to be ranked "with the chiefest of those men of God who were Israel's unique gift to the world."[1] His name is among the truly great of all time, but it must ever be spoken with a certain overtone that carries the faith and hope and love of one of humanity's noblest mothers.

MARY, MOTHER OF JESUS

Jesus' Birth at Bethlehem

With devotion and reverence we follow the shepherds and wisemen to the manger at Bethlehem. Simplicity of faith that confounds both doubt and fear is ours as we enter the sacred portal. Whatever of worth or power our personalities may hold as treasure, we offer in worshipful consecration. Here the mystery of the ages is revealed. The infinite love of God fills all of life about us and within.

> And the Word became flesh, and dwelt among us (and we beheld his glory, glory as of the only begotten of the Father), full of grace and truth.[2]

Matthew and Luke set forth the events that led up to the journey of Joseph and Mary to Bethlehem, and vividly describe the conditions attendant upon the birth of the Saviour.[3] The decree of Caesar Augustus that a census be taken throughout the empire was tempered by a certain respect for the manners and customs of the peoples in the various areas of the realm. Among the Hebrews the locale of a person's citizenship was not of necessity his place of

[1] Fleming James, *op. cit.*, p. 95.
[2] John 1:14.
[3] Matt. 1:18—2; Like 1—2:40. Familiar as these accounts are, they should be read again with special attention to the details that bear upon the theme of our study.

17

birth, residence, or employment. Rather was it the seat of his ancient tribal and clan possession. Thus it behooved those of "the lineage of David" to register at Bethlehem no matter where they might then reside.[1] Those of other descent, notable or obscure, must perforce similarly travel across the land to the place of their own ancestral relationship. There was much coming and going, and doubtless in many towns great confusion, as the countless individuals and families moved north, south, east, and west, those days just preceding the due date for the official registration.

Those who actually lived in their place of citizenship were, by that chance, most fortunate. A family with only a short distance to travel could readily find some accommodation with friends. When a small town of that day had to receive a host of travelers because of the unexpected numbers of its legal citizens from afar, there was crowding and hardship. Men and women, faced with a journey nearly the north-south length of the land in extent, and having to swing east of the Jordan and back again to avoid Samaria, held little chance of any place to stay save some corner in the public caravansary, or even in the open fields. And when travel must be made slowly for physical reasons, there could be no room in any house and possibly only a cattle-stall available for rest and privacy.

The last forty miles of Mary's journey were cruel. They involved the sharp descent from the uplands east of Jordan to the low level of the river's plain. Then came the trail across the heat-stricken desert stretch at over a thousand feet below sea-level, fording the Jordan and reaching Jericho. The terrific Jericho road still lay ahead, climbing and twisting through the indescribable bad-lands, ever upward from the thousand feet below sea-level, to thirty-five

[1]Luke 2:3-5.

18

hundred feet above, at the crest of Olivet overlooking Jerusalem. Brigand-infested, steep, stony, tortuous, without water from Jericho to the inn later to be made famous by the Saviour's immortal parable,[1] it was difficult enough for hardy men. What must it have been to Mary scarce three days before her hour of sacrament in the stable. But she held God's promise close in her heart, and there was Bethlehem ahead. She was to know the hushed quiet of animals that understood, a faithful man's strong arms, and the cooling water from David's own well close at hand.[2] A manger of stone was there for the baby's bed.[3] And the Son of God was brought to birth.

A few quiet days at Bethlehem came when the registration was done, and the crowds began to melt back to their distant homes. The Babe was presented at the Temple at Jerusalem only five miles away. Just as Joseph thought Mary to be strong enough to travel back to Nazareth, the eastern Magi completed their pilgrimage of adoration. And in their wake there echoed the stride of jealous Herod's soldiers to strike and kill.[4] The swift flight to Egypt along the ancient coastal road on which the caravans of the continents ever moved was made possible in the value of the wisemen's kingly gifts. So fled Joseph and Mary and the Babe—these Displaced Persons—these Royal Refugees.

The Family at Nazareth

Joseph and Mary had had their home in Nazareth where Joseph was an experienced carpenter. Upon the death of Herod, the family was at liberty to return from the exile in

---

[1]Luke 10:25-37.

[2]Read the story of how David's warriors fetched a skin of water from this very well when he was athirst in the heat of battle (II Sam. 23:13-17).

[3]A stone manger from Bethlehem is enshrined in the Hanson Place—Central Methodist Church, Brooklyn, New York.

[4]Matt. 2:16-18.

19

Egypt. Jesus was a toddling boy when they made the journey and re-established themselves in the old home environment. A second son was soon born, whom they called James. Other children came, three more boys and at least two girls.[1]

Joseph knew hard and constant toil to maintain such a home, feeding and clothing the seven children, paying the heavy taxes, both governmental and religious, carrying his work as a carpenter. Mary's burdens were likewise heavy. The intimate duties of the household were hers, together with the teaching of the group of eager active children. The school attached to the local synagogue undoubtedly did much for Jesus and James, the two oldest boys. But the training of all of them in human relationships, whether among themselves or with others in the towns, was chiefly Mary's task. She could do more than all others to translate the letter of the Law that the boys absorbed at the synagogue-school into the vital actuality of daily righteous living. She and Joseph, alike, were of unusually devout spirit. This attitude they sedulously cultivated in the children. The prayer life of the Saviour and the Church's later application of the title "The Just" to James for his uprightness, were accolades that Joseph and Mary might truly wear in high honor.

Although born at Bethlehem, Jesus thus lived in Nazareth until he entered upon his ministry. There was a vast difference between the towns as places wherein to grow. To be a lad in Nazareth, to see each day the sites of tremendous historic events spread out in a panorama at one's feet, to know intimately the great roads focusing on the plain below the town as they tied together the commerce of the

---

[1]Matt. 13:55, 56; Mark 6:3—where the names of Jesus' four brothers appear, and the word for sisters is in the plural.

continents, to glimpse the blue Mediterranean beyond Carmel's thrusting cape and watch the moving ships, great grain-laden triremes from Egypt, swift cutters of Rome's Navy—this was the Saviour's privilege. Bethlehem, on a side road, distant from the coast, with no far-traveling caravans, could offer only a narrow provincialism as a meaning for life.

At Nazareth, also, there was a sense of freedom in the very air one breathed. This was Galilee of the Nations. Here men's hopes beat high. Here every revolt against tyranny was engendered, and had its brave support. That these heroic efforts seemed ever doomed to fail proved no deterrent to the men in whose hearts the spirit of the Maccabees still lived. At Bethlehem Jesus would have breathed the fetid air of political appeasement of Rome, of the compromising acquiescence for the sake of a little futile power, that so saturated Jerusalem.

Jesus was no revolutionary, and he carefully kept himself from any contact with the political underground. That was not his method, and the torch and sword were never his weapons. Yet, when he stood in heated argument at Jerusalem with the betrayers of freedom who boastingly shouted, "We are Abraham's seed, and have never yet been in bondage to any man,"[1] a clarion of liberty, as from his home in the hills of Galilee, sounded in his reply: "If therefore the Son shall make you free, ye shall be free indeed."[2]

As in politics and government, so was it also in matters of religious faith and practice. The Temple crowned Jerusalem, and Bethlehem rested in its shadow. Truly this must be the holy place. As a lad of twelve Jesus came to it with his parents, and he tarried there in eager boyish search for

[1]John 8:33.
[2]John 8:36.

the truth of God.[1] Yet he was to find that truth, not at the Temple, but in perfect clarity on the hillcrest above Nazareth. He was to learn its application to life day by day under Mary's wise instruction, and as he saw it enacted and made a living power in the life of Joseph. There was the possibility of a spiritual freedom in Nazareth unknown at Bethlehem. It was "the prophet, Jesus from Nazareth of Galilee,"[2] as men were to call him, who said to the woman at the well near Sychar:

> Woman, believe me, the hour cometh, when neither in this mountain, nor in Jerusalem, shall ye worship the Father . . . . . But the hour cometh, and now is, when the true worshippers shall worship the Father in spirit and truth: for such doth the Father seek to be his worshippers.[3]

These are some of the facts whose light and color filled the soul of the boy Jesus as he grew to manhood at Nazareth. It is not known whether he was more influenced by the world about him, or by the vital approach to the ancient Scriptures and to the great ideas concerning God, and men, and his own race that he gained at the synagogue-school; however, the most powerful forces at play in the development of his spirit were the piety, faith, and righteousness of Joseph and Mary. These were paramount as he came to that amazing maturity of spiritual thought by which he has ever been known, and to that relationship with others which we call "Jesus' way of life."

The Character of Mary

From the instant that she knew she was to be the mother of the Saviour, to that last vision we have of her as a quiet, devout member of the group of believers, Mary is to us the epitome of consecration and service. She knew a joy far

[1]Luke 2:41-50.
[2]Matt. 21:11.
[3]John 4:21, 23.

22

more profound than words can say, albeit there may have been a cruel misunderstanding and shame at the first, as well as an indescribable sorrow at the close, of her Son's earthly life. Suffering, toil, pain, and a trascendant peace of mind, and utter confidence in God merged so completely that the purity of heart, the kindness of spirit, the wisdom of judgment, and the strength for daily living that she evidenced seem unique.

Spiritual intuition of great depth was hers, and a moral fiber of tremendous strength and power. The secret of these possessions she gave unstintedly to the Saviour. The duties and humble tasks of the home were sedulously carried out. A love was in her heart so broad and beautiful that it encircled all seven children, and Joseph, and a wider range of friends, without taint of favoritism for Jesus, or James, or any other. Widowed comparatively early, she gave herself tirelessly to the care of her children, with the support that Jesus and James could provide. She moved in a calm sense of personal dignity, yet with a restraint that is remarkable. Even after the Resurrection and the glory of her Son, we note no trace of forwardness or pride. She was simply one of the believers, honored and beloved truly, but in no vaunted position of grandeur. In the records we possess there is no mention of her passing. Yet, she lived long enough to have been able to give to Luke the intimate details of her own experience and of the Saviour's life that he alone relates.[1]

> Every touch in the Gospels concerning the life at Nazareth, every implied allusion to it, brings up a picture of goodness and truth—and a parental care for a growing boy, shared by two who both could hear angels speak, and who both desired only the rightful purposes of God.[2]

[1] This appears to have been done when he was Paul's companion during the apostle's imprisonment at Caesarea.
[2] Lady Hosie, *Jesus and Woman* (London: Hodder & Stoughton, 1947), p. 273. Used by permission of the author.

Luke phrases it in words of simple, radiant beauty that are unequaled:

> And he went down with them, and came to Nazareth; and he was subject unto them: and his mother kept all these sayings in her heart. And Jesus advanced in wisdom and stature, and in favor with God and men . . . . . and the grace of God was upon him.[1]

[1]Luke 2:51,52, 40.

SUGGESTIONS FOR FURTHER STUDY

1. Study the following biblical references to Sarah: Isaiah 51:1-3; Romans 9:6-13; Hebrews 11:8-12; I Peter 3:1-6. Note how her faith in God is placed on an equality of spiritual power with that of Abraham. If you observe any primary traits of her character indicated in these passages that are additional to those in the account of her life in Genesis, state what they are.

2. Read the story of Rebekah in Genesis 24 to 27; also the accounts of her twin sons, continued through Genesis 35. She had had no training as a child in the faith and service of Jehovah, as had Isaac her husband. Was this a handicap or an advantage to her in rearing their sons, Esau and Jacob? Consider whether the dominant personal traits of the two —Esau, a sullen, non-social aloofness; Jacob, a selfish, unprincipled craftiness—may have been initiated and developed by her very evident partiality for one of them as against the other.

3. The record of Jacob's journey to the east, and of his taking Leah and Rachel to wife, is found in Genesis, chapter 29 and following. Read these chapters, making note of the characters of Leah and Rachel as they develop. Their sons were to constitute the fathers of the Twelve Tribes of Israel. What did their mothers give them as heritage, and in training? Were they better off in religious training than Esau and Jacob had been with Rebekah?

4. Despite the fact that Samuel, as a priest, offered countless sacrifices for the people, consider his utterance to Saul upon the king's disobedience of God's command:

> Hath Jehovah as great delight in burnt offerings and sacrifices, as in obeying the voice of Jehovah? Behold, to obey is better than sacrifice, and to hearken than the fat of rams. (Sam. 15:22)

Study these later prophetic declarations: Psalms 40:6-8;

51:16, 17; Isaiah 1:14-17; 8:6; Amos 5:21-24; Hosea 6:6; Mark 12:13. Judge how far Samuel may have influenced these statements.

5. Read Proverbs 31:10-31, noting carefully the characteristics of this "ideal woman" of the ancient wise man. What elements would you alter, or what other traits would you add, to portray the Christian ideal of woman?

Chapter Two

Sharing the Blessings
of the Home

IN THE PRECEDING CHAPTER our thought was devoted to the inter-relationships of those who constitute the home, particularly to the significance of careful religious training of the little ones who may be the home's chief joy. The family was considered primarily in terms of the ties and intimacies that make of it a closely knit group. The family, however, is much like a person. Each of us has two reciprocal aspects of life. Every man or woman is, first, an individual in his own right—personally responsible for his compelling motives, choices, habits, and the conduct that flows therefrom. Yet, each is also a social being whose life is inextricably interwoven with a multitude of other personal beings like himself. And the tests whereby we judge ourselves and others as individuals are representative of what we have together socially established as wise or foolish, practical or visionary, right or wrong.

So, also, is it of a family. The group in the home is like a coin. Both sides, obverse and reverse, must be fully minted before the coin can pass into circulation at its true value. There is an intimate, individual existence each home possesses in its own inherent right. There is also a vaster total with which it stands in close organic relationship. From society as a whole, each family unit draws tremendously for security and resources of every sort. To this greater sphere each small circle should give of its highest and noblest. We shall, accordingly, consider some of the ways in which the family shares life with others, noting how religion in the heart may lift that sharing to the high level of the kingdom of God.

These widening contacts of the home constitute some of life's finest privileges. The ramifying ties of kindred and the broadening angles of friendship add to the mutually developing pattern of the family's relationships with others. Countless opportunities present themselves for gracious hospitality to those who come and go. Often, persons in the home evidence professional skill or social and cultural gifts that open the way to places of genuine leadership in the larger community. With the understanding and inspiring confidence of his family, the talented one offers far richer treasure to society than if he must simply "go it alone." And the home, in its turn, inherits a wealth of joyous experience in the triumph and services of the loved one. Citizenship is a privilege and function of the individual. The family, however, gains much from the nation by virtue of the rights of citizenship each member enjoys, and owes an obligation in accordance.

Each of us treasures, though in varying degree, the sanctity of our moments of private devotion. And, when these are reinforced by the worship and the service of the family, a gracious blessing of very great potency comes into life. In turn, the corporate worth of the Church—the living, acting body of the Lord—binds together such as come to it, of the many otherwise separated experiences of the individual and his family, into an organic whole surcharged with tremendous moral and spiritual vitality. We here note only some of the factors that operate in the widening of the contacts of the family. Let the reader add such others as he himself has experienced.

THE HOSPITALITY OF A NAMELESS WIDOW

Two simple incidents recorded in the Old Testament show the worth of kindly hospitality in a truly beauteous light. One took place at Zarephath, near Sidon, today known as Sarepta.[1] Famine stalked the land because of the seering drought proclaimed by Elijah in the name of Jehovah. Pursued by Jezebel's fury, driven to seek safety beyond the borders of Ahab's power, the prophet, guided by the divine Spirit, came to Zarephath. There the nameless widow, whose larder held but a scanty handful of meal and a little oil, and whose only son was famished almost to death, nevertheless gave to Elijah the small cake he asked:

> And she went and did according to the saying of Elijah: and she, and he, and her house, did eat many days. The jar of meal wasted not, neither did the cruse of oil fail, according to the word of Jehovah, which he spake by Elijah.[2]

So significant was this hospitality during grievous famine, and in the light of their racial difference—she a Sidonian, he a Hebrew—that the Saviour spoke of it at Nazareth in these notable words:

> There were many widows in Israel in the days of Elijah, when the heaven was shut up three years and six months, when there came a great famine over all the land; and unto none of them was Elijah sent, but only to Zarephath in the land of Sidon, unto a woman that was a widow.[3]

This incident brings to mind that other widow Jesus himself saw giving her two mites to the Temple treasury out of her heart's devotion to God:

> And he said, Of a truth I say unto you, This poor widow cast in more than they all: for all these did of their superfluity cast in unto the gifts; but she of her want did cast in all the living that she had.[4]

---

[1] I Kings 17:1-24.
[2] I Kings 17:15,16.
[3] Luke 4:25,26.
[4] Luke 21:3,4 (Mark 12:41-44).

THE SHUNAMMITE WOMAN

The other incident occurred in the work of Elisha.[1] The prophet frequently passed through Shunem, a town close to the imposing fortress of Jezreel. Elisha was deeply loved by all sorts of folk who could always depend on his sympathetic understanding and selfless love. As he came and went on his itinerary, one of the prominent families of Shunem offered special hospitality. The wife in this home of wealth had come to sense the abiding value of Elisha's work among the people. She caught the vision of its spiritual meaning. She suggested to her husband that they offer to Elisha the facility of a new and quiet room they would be glad to build for him, as an addition to their own home. Here the prophet might find rest and comfort according to his need. Elisha gladly accepted the courtesy of his friends, thus making their home the center of his ministry in that area. The warm friendship that developed was rich in mutual helpfulness and spiritual blessing, especially in the tragic sorrow that soon entered this kindly home. And in the community, the man of God blessed many in need because of the thoughtfulness of this woman and her husband.

These ancient happenings demonstrate how poverty and wealth alike may find the incalculable riches of divine blessing in the simple acts of human consideration and homely courtesy. And when the contacts thus established are illumined and warmed by religious faith, they come to possess both an immediacy of meaning and a lambent glow that even the long years cannot dim.

---

[1] II Kings 4:8-14.

CONTRIBUTION OF HOMES TO
JESUS' MINISTRY

Capernaum, located on the northern shore of the Sea of Galilee, was an important city in Jesus' day. At that point the very ancient through-road from Egypt and the coast to Damascus and the farther East crossed a Roman province boundary. The customs collection post on such a road at such a boundary would rank high in the network of imperial tax-control. Other roads radiated from Capernaum—one eastward around the lake, another southward to Tiberias and the busy fishing towns beyond, a third north-westward towards Roman Sepphoris, Tyre, and Sidon. Thus Capernaum was a center of industry, government, tax-control, and radiating commerce. It was with true appraisal of its importance that Jesus made it focal to his highly significant Galilean ministry.

Rebuffed at Nazareth where he had grown up, thrust out of the synagogue where as a lad he had received much training in the ancient Scriptures, the Saviour found a far more friendly reception at Capernaum.[1] Here was possible a richer, warmer fellowship with the fisher-folk than with the men of the very Nazareth guild of carpenters wherein he and Joseph before him had held membership. The brothers who were to become his disciples, Peter and Andrew, John and James, made him welcome in their homes, and the women of the households eagerly offered their devotion and service to meet the Saviour's need. Levi Matthew, who held a post in Rome's custom-house of such importance that he was "sitting at the place of toll,"[2] entertained him with

---

[1] Luke 4:16-37.
[2] Luke 5:27-32; parallels in Matthew and Mark.

31

a large number of friends. Following that dinner, Matthew joined the group of Jesus' close disciples.[1]

In contrast with the situation in Nazareth, none of these were ashamed to own their friendship and allegiance to the Master. All Capernaum knew their love for Jesus. Indeed, one household, probably Peter's, received him so intimately that Mark, recording his presence there, uses the colloquial Greek phrase for our "at home" to describe the situation.

> And when he entered again into Capernaum after some days, it was noised that he was at home.[2]

Immediately the incident follows of the palsied man whose friends were so persistent in their desire that Jesus heal him that they removed some of the roof tiles, unrebuked by the host, and lowered the sick man into Jesus' very presence.

Such a home as this in Capernaum offered genuine hospitality to the Saviour. But those of the home also eagerly shared him with the entire community. We must always remember that back of this sharing was the love and devotion of the women of the household. The crowding of the throngs, the disruption of normal schedules, the curious and insistent questioning of friends for days afterwards, to say nothing of the disturbance to the house itself, laid a heavy physical and nervous toll on Peter's wife and her ageing mother. Not only did they carry this load; they also gladly made the necessary great adjustments when Peter and Andrew laid down the nets and pulled the boats unto the shore as they prepared to follow the Master. This sharing demanded greatly of them all. They made the tremendous sacrifice because of their deep love for the Saviour. Together with the mother of John and James, and the unnamed woman of Matthew's household, these of Peter's home

---

[1] It is judged that the words of Jesus as recorded by Matthew are as close to the actual utterances as we can hope to come.

[2] This is the marginal reading (equivalent of the French "chez lui").

were the first of an uncounted throng in all ages and lands who have taken him so closely to their hearts that he is "at home" with them. And then they have opened wide the door to share him with their friends and with all men.

THE HOME OF MARY OF JERUSALEM

Somewhere in that section of Jerusalem frequented by people from Galilee and the north when on pilgrimage, there stood a commodious house whose doors were open to many friends from afar. The head of the household was a widow named Mary, and she had a young son called John Mark. The lad was to become the companion of his cousin Barnabas and Paul on the first missionary journey. Later John Mark was the companion of Barnabas alone, then of Peter, again of Paul; he was also a close friend of Luke, Silas, and Timothy. He was the author of the Gospel bearing his name.

There were intimate family relationships with groups on the island of Cyprus, and probably also in or near Antioch, the famous city of Syria. Barnabas of Cyprus, who was so closely associated with Paul after his conversion and with the church at Antioch, was Mary's nephew.

Mary of Jerusalem was a woman of social position. We do not know her husband's name, or anything about his business, but at his death he had evidently left her with abundant provision for every need. The house was large, with a spacious upper room approached by an outer stairway,[1] and there was a retinue of servants. There were deeply religious susceptibilities in this household, and probably some connections with a group in the Sanhedrin and at the Temple, of which Nicodemus and Joseph of

[1]See EBL—article "Stone Houses," pp. 242-246; and illust. between pp. 238 and 239.

Arimathea were typical. The son, John Mark, though bereft of his father in his early teens, possessed the heritage of culture and refinement, of faith and devotion, that has ever been as a halo about his home.

The Gospels do not indicate when the friendship began between this lovely home and Jesus and his disciples. It must have been early enough for a beautiful intimacy to have been established before the last testing week of the Saviour's life. To this home the disciples were guided to prepare for the Passover meal. Here the immortal sayings recorded by John were spoken,[1] and the sacrament we call the Holy Communion was instituted by the Saviour.[2] The hospitality extended by Mary of Jerusalem was so warm and genuine and the foundation of friendship so firm and sincere, that her "upper room" was the natural place for Jesus and his disciples to complete their Passover observance. It was ever to be a sacred memory to Mary and her son that their home was the last the blessed Master knew!

> And when they had sung a hymn, they went out unto the mount of Olives. . . . . And they came unto a place which was called Gethsemane: and he saith unto his disciples, Sit ye here while I pray. . . . . And he saith unto them, My soul is exceeding sorrowful even unto death: abide ye here, and watch.[3]

Mary of Jerusalem and the circle of her acquaintance had given much to the Saviour. There was always a warmth of welcome and a genteel kindliness that strengthened him after the difficult moments of debate at the Temple, and in the loneliness that seemed to dog his steps in the Holy City. A careful reading of the Gospels will show how constantly in Galilee the homes of all sorts of people were open to the Saviour. He spent many serene and joyous hours in such circles of quiet friendship. In the Jerusalem area, however,

[1]John 13 through 17.
[2]Mark 14:14-25, and parallels in the other Gospels.
[3]Mark 14:26, 32, 34.

there seem to have been only two where he might reasonably feel at home—this of Mary in the city; and that of Martha, Mary, and Lazarus at Bethany.[1] And in the last desperate night and the awful agony of Calvary, his courage was renewed, and his power to withstand was undergirded in the memory of the peace and lovely fellowship of this blessed home. Mary and her faithful household had shared with the Master in such a way that his suffering was a bit easier to bear and his triumph more definitely assured by reason of the loving devotion wherewith they had surrounded him.

The First Home of the Early Church

Within a very few hours word of the Resurrection had spread among the wider range of the disciples. There was incredulity and disbelief on the part of some, matched by wonderment and joyful anticipation in the hearts of all. Great fear of the authorities and of the rabble still gripped them, for they could never forget the terrible course of events from Thursday night into Friday. But this amazing story of Mark, of the women, of Peter and John, overcame all else. Rumors of the strict disciplining of the guard that had been stationed at the tomb sped through the city. The curious ventured out to look at the tomb, but many kept away lest they be charged with complicity in the stealing of his body.

Wherever the disciples may have lodged in the city, whether with relatives or friends, or at one of the hostels established for pilgrims, the home of Mary of Jerusalem was their rallying point. On Easter evening the Eleven, save only Thomas, were assembled there with as many more as could crowd into the sacred upper room where the

---

[1]The influence of the Bethany household is discussed later in this chapter.

bread had been broken and the cup had been passed. The doors were shut,[1] and some security established against possible marauders. Into the midst came the two from Emmaus who told in these memorable words of the glory they had experienced:

> Was not our heart burning within us, while he spake to us in the way, while he opened to us the scriptures? .... And they rehearsed the things that happened in the way, and how he was known of them in the breaking of the bread.[2]

And immediately

> He himself stood in the midst of them, and saith unto them, Peace be unto you. . . . .[3] as the Father hath sent me, even so send I you . . . . . Receive ye the Holy Spirit . . . . .[4] Ye are witnesses of these things. And behold, I send forth the promise of my Father upon you: but tarry ye in the city, until ye be clothed with power from on high.[5]

Faith and vital experience banished doubt and incredulity. Fear no longer shadowed them in the streets. There was light, and a song, and "joy unspeakable and full of glory."[6] The solemn words spoken by the Saviour in this room on Thursday night began to glow in their hearts with unsuspected meaning. The broken bread and the wine in the cup became to them a veritable sacrament—his living presence to cleanse and empower. How sacred the place where these events transpired—this upper room in the home of Mary of Jerusalem!

Came another eight days, and in this same room Thomas resolved all doubt into overwhelming faith as he cried, "My Lord and my God."[7] There was ecstasy and praise. The disciples were ever in the Temple, and then back

---

[1] John 20:19.
[2] Luke 24:32, 35.
[3] Luke 24:36.
[4] John 20:21, 22.
[5] Luke 24:48, 49 (Acts 1:1-5).
[6] I Pet. 1:8.
[7] John 20:24-29.

again in the upper room for quiet counsel. A sense of destiny
dawned and grew among them. A mission in the world
began to loom. Finally came the awesome moment when
the Risen Lord departed from them as "a cloud received
him out of their sight."[1] His words were ever to live in
their hearts:

> Ye shall receive power when the Holy Spirit is come upon you:
> and ye shall be my witnesses both in Jerusalem, and in all Judaea and
> Samaria, and unto the uttermost part of the earth.[2]
>
> Then returned they unto Jerusalem from the mount called Olivet,
> which is nigh unto Jerusalem, a sabbath day's journey off. And when
> they were come in, they went up into the upper chamber, where
> they were abiding.[3]

Pentecost and After

Day after day, night after night, the apostolic group moved
in and out of this sacred room in the devoted home of Mary
and John Mark. They elected a qualified disciple to take the
place of Judas Iscariot among The Twelve. They tarried in
constant prayer until the Day of Pentecost, when the Spirit
of the Risen Lord descended upon them all in transcendent
power. Times without number the believers met in the
upper room of Mary's house. Uncounted people passed
through the doorway into the warmth and protection of
this home. One occasion is still to be noted in our study.
There were hours of great anxiety, moments of shocking
sorrow for those of the Jerusalem Church. Saul of Tarsus
wrought havoc among them, and the deathless roll of
Christian martyrs was begun with the stoning of Stephen.
Somewhat later Herod Agrippa, seeking to please a powerful clique of the leading Jews, caused the death of James, the
apostle, brother of John, son of Zebedee. Then he seized
Peter, imprisoning him with the expectation of making his

[1]Acts 1:9.
[2]Acts 1:8.
[3]Acts 1:12,13.

punishment a public spectacle after the days of the Passover. Luke vividly reports these incidents, and the miraculous escape of Peter.[1] Through the unlighted twisting streets of the ancient city, the apostle made his way unerringly to the home of Mary. There the faithful were gathered in all-night prayer for him—for his safety and deliverance, if that were possible, for his abiding faith and tenacity of spirit whatever might occur. To their stupified amazement Rhoda, one of Mary's loyal maids, announced Peter's escape from prison, and his lusty pounding at the gate but emphasized his freedom. Here was safety, if only for a short hour. But also here, in Mary's home, was the pulsing heart of the Church, and Peter left vital messages for James, the Lord's brother, who was already recognized as the leader in Jerusalem.

Years had passed for Mary of Jerusalem since first she welcomed Jesus of Nazareth and his Galilean disciples. She had shared substance with them in that gracious hospitality that adds much of light and beauty to life. Then the Saviour had shared with her, and with her young son, his faith in God and his saving grace. With the glorious enrichment of his love she ever gave more and more to others. Her upper room became a shrine of faith and worship, an altar of sacramental glory. Her home was a refuge for harried people who fled the wrath of rulers or the insatiate fury of the mob. Her own brave soul was strength to them, and the fidelity and courage of her retinue protected many. Then, at last, with great joy she offered the supreme sharing of her home as her nephew

> Barnabas and Saul returned to Antioch from Jerusalem, when they had fulfilled their ministration, taking with them John whose surname was Mark.[2]

[1]Acts 12:1-19.
[2]Acts 12:25.

38

After long years this same Paul, tired and broken in body, languishing in the penetrating dampness of his final imprisonment at Rome, but still of indomitable faith and undiminished spiritual power, wrote to Timothy, his tireless coadjutor:

> Give diligence to come shortly unto me. . . . . Only Luke is with me. Take Mark, and bring him with thee; for he is useful to me for ministering. . . . . bring when thou comest . . . . the books, especially the parchments.[1]

Thus we see the great Apostle to the Gentiles, in the company of three treasured helpers, planning the abiding strategy of the Church, studying the priceless manuscripts, praying, and serving. With Luke, his beloved physician, Timothy, his son in the gospel, there stands beside Paul in these last days John Mark, whose presence brings again precious memory of a lovely home that never ceased to share, and of a queenly mother, beloved and revered, Mary of Jerusalem.

PAUL AT LYSTRA

It was a long time since Paul had come first to Lystra, tucked away among the rugged mountains of interior Asia Minor.[2] He and Barnabas had been set apart by the church at Antioch in Syria for such a mission, and they had gone forth with the earnest prayer and eager hope of that first mission-minded congregation. After itinerating through Cyprus, Barnabas' native island, they crossed to the mainland of Asia Minor, striking directly into the interior. At Pisidian Antioch[3] and Iconium measurable success was achieved, but bitter opposition also developed. Moving eastward along the one major road, they came to Lystra and

---

[1]II Tim. 4:9, 11, 13.
[2]Acts 14:8 ff.
[3]This city must never be confused with the Antioch in Syria from which they had set forth.

after that to Derbe, two smaller cities quite close together with much in common.

LOIS, EUNICE, AND TIMOTHY

In vivid terms Luke relates several visits that Paul made to Lystra.[1] On the development of opposition at Pisidian Antioch and Iconium, Paul and Barnabas had come to Lystra. Here Paul had found a Jewish family consisting of elderly Lois, her widowed daughter, Eunice, and her son, Timothy, a young man of unusual personality and devotion. Despite the fact that there was no synagogue in Lystra, and that Eunice had married a Greek, Timothy had been closely schooled by Lois and Eunice in the reading and interpretation of the Jewish Scriptures. They undoubtedly possessed the Septuagint text,[2] which in its Greek form was widely used among the Jews of the Dispersion. Paul shows marked familiarity with this text of the Old Testament, and evidence indicates that he employed it constantly in his preaching.

Under Paul's inspiring appeal this family accepted the Saviour and crowned their earlier fidelity to God by this acknowledgment of Jesus as his Son and as their Lord and Master. They saw Paul stoned and lying unconscious in the pool of his own blood. They knew the bitter suffering of other Christians in the neighboring churches; and they doubtless bore their own marks of persecution. Yet they remained faithful, and grew in zeal and devotion. On a later day, Paul, with Silas, revisited the churches in this area, counseling them in their problems of administration, con-

[1]Acts 14:1-28; 16:1-5.

[2]This Greek version of the ancient Hebrew text had been made several generations before the birth of Jesus for the use of those Jews scattered over the Roman world who spoke Greek, and had lost the classical Hebrew. We call it the "Septuagint" from the Greek word representing the Seventy elders who had made the translation.

firming them in faith and service. This was his habit throughout the long apostolic ministry he was destined to give to the Church—revisiting the local congregations as opportunity might offer, keeping in constant correspondence with them, continuing instant in love and service with them.

The Consecration of Timothy

Timothy had so grown in grace and developed in ability that his reputation in leadership was exemplary throughout the churches of this wide area. Thus, when Paul returned with Silas, he found Timothy ready and eager to join his company. The churches approved his desire. Lois and Eunice gave him to this service with "unfeigned faith"[1] and profound joy, albeit they knew that danger lay directly ahead and would constantly be his companion. Laying his hands upon him, Paul ordained Timothy for this office of service and sacrifice.

The three then left Lystra—Paul, Silas, and Timothy— for that journey overland to Troas, and then across the Aegean to Philippi and the organization of the first branch of the Church of Christ on the continent of Europe. There Timothy was to tarry with Luke, who had joined them at Troas, aiding in the establishment of that powerful congregation. Ever with Paul, or acting for him and with his authority among the various churches, Timothy served for many years as one of the most illustrious ministers of the apostolic group. He himself knew suffering, hardship, and even imprisonment,[2] but always the grace of God was with him. So rich was the influence of his devout mother and grandmother that their prayers and love were ever his

---

[1]II Tim. 1:5.
[2]The author of Hebrews reports to the Church with gladness that Timothy had been released. (Heb. 13:23.)

as a veritable aura beautifying his own noble character. As devout Jewish women they had shared God's truth with the cherished lad, and as consecrated Christians they shared him with the living Church. Their spirit abides deathless in the inspiration we today may take from Timothy's loyalty, untarnished devotion, and tireless service.

HOME OF PRISCILLA

At Athens, seat of culture, beauty, and wisdom, Paul suffered as bitter a disappointment as appears anywhere in his career as an apostle. The dilettante sceptics and cultured sophisticates of the world's intellectual capital hurt him profoundly, not so much for his own sake as for the Saviour's. Paul did not so much care that, in their polished slang, they called him "a strange bird picking up stray seeds."[1] He did care that they would ruthlessly subject the immortal glory of the Saviour's resurrection and his imperial ethical demands to the distorting analysis of their dialectic. Soon after the public utterance on Mars Hill,[2] Paul left Athens for the more violent experiences, but far more fertile field, of Corinth.

Corinth was one of the most amazing cities in all the Roman world. Into and out of its harbor there moved a greater total of ships and a vaster tonnage than any other port east of Italy save possibly only Alexandria in Egypt. It lay southwest from Athens across the bay, and from the portico of the beautiful little Temple of Victory on the Acropolis, one could see the white sails off Corinth's headland like so many seagulls awing in the distance.

A glance at the map of Greece will show the strategic location of the city on the Isthmus connecting the Greek

---

[1] A literal rendering of the Greek slang word translated "babbler" (Acts 17:18).

[2] Acts 17:22-31.

Peloponnesus with the total of Europe. From the Adriatic Sea on the west the long, narrow, and deep Gulf of Corinth thrusts itself between these land masses straight eastward to the Isthmus. Here lies Corinth athwart the Isthmus, a scant five miles wide. A railroad had been built on whose wooden cars, pulled by slaves, whole ships with all their cargo were regularly trundled from sea to sea. Thus the wild winds and tempestuous waters off the southern capes of Greece could be avoided.[1] The only road connecting the north and south of Greece passed along the Isthmus through Corinth. Thus the city stood at the crossroads of the vast traffic of the Eastern Mediterranean.

Its population was polyglot and interracial to an intense degree. There was a constantly shifting transient crowd of sailors, tradesmen, adventurers, from every corner of the known world. So morally debased and profligate was the life of Corinth, that the very name of the city had become a byword for depravity.[2] To this teeming, seething, brawling, vile, and ribald city, Paul came to found the Church of Christ. The measure of his success may be gauged by this salutation in his first letter to that church written at a later date from Ephesus:

> . . . . unto the church of God which is at Corinth, even them that are sanctified in Christ Jesus, called to be saints, ...[3]

Aquila and Priscilla Ministering to Paul

Come to Corinth after the disillusioning experience of effete Athens, Paul felt the sheer necessity of sturdy physical effort.[4] And his scanty funds doubtless needed replenishing. He sought out his craft guild, the weavers of tent cloth.

---

[1] Paul was later to know the fury of storms in this area (Acts 27:1-44).

[2] To say that a person "lived like a Corinthian" was to pass the deadly insult for which blows might well be struck.

[3] I Cor. 1:2.

[4] Acts 18:1-4.

Lately arrived from Rome and member of the craft was Aquila, with his wife Priscilla. He was a Jew, native of Pontus, where he had learned his craft as a lad. Reaching Rome on business he had married Priscilla.[1] The recent edict of Claudius banishing all Jews from the Imperial City had forced them out. They had found refuge in Corinth where Aquila resumed his craft. Although displaced persons themselves, these hospitable people opened their home and establishment to Paul, offering him, a stranger, employment, lodging, and the warmth of congenial fellowship. They toiled together, living in cramped quarters of Corinth's workers, thrusting the clumsy spindles back and forth on the loom as the heavy tent cloth[2] grew in bulk and weight under their skilled hands. In his moments of comparative leisure, Paul sought the synagogue, or the concourse of those who would listen, as he "preached the unsearchable riches of Christ."[3] This was his life for nearly two years in Corinth.

Luke does not indicate whether Aquila and Priscilla had professed faith in Christ while at Rome, or whether they were the first fruits of Paul's preaching at Corinth. However it was, their home and their enterprise were his without question or stint. This human virtue of kindly hospitality ennobles much of life at every level of culture and social order. When its ardor is blessed by the gentle grace of religious faith, there is richness and value far beyond the merely human aspect. Whether as devout Jews or as earnest Christians, Aquila and Priscilla welcomed Paul, and the friendship thus begun was to develop across

[1]Her name may indicate Roman ancestry.
[2]The material woven of goat's hair was called cilicium after Paul's native Province, Cilicia. See articles in EBL, pp. 238; 353-355.
[3]Eph. 3:8.

the years into a comradeship of mutual service and tested loyalty.

Aquila and Priscilla at Ephesus

When the church had been firmly rooted at Corinth, Paul felt constrained to go to Jerusalem. He decided to travel by way of Ephesus.[1] Having business there at the same time, Aquila and Priscilla went with him. Apparently they settled with a certain permanence, for Paul was to find them still at Ephesus, eagerly at work with the church, when he returned after a prolonged mission confirming the disciples in Galatia and Phrygia.

During this time the brilliant young Alexandrean Jew, Apollos, had come to Ephesus.[2] He was well trained in the Hellenistic philosophy of that Egyptian center of culture, but he had also accepted the baptism of John the Baptist and was thus possessed of a rudimentary concept of Jesus as the world's Saviour. Noting his unusual gifts—a profound knowledge of the Scriptures, an ordered philosophy of life, a rare eloquence—Priscilla and Aquila[3] took him to their home "and expounded unto him the way of God more accurately."[4]

Following this training by his new friends, Apollos went to Corinth where he built most effectively upon the foundation Paul had laid.[5] Later, he returned to Ephesus, but declined to go again to Corinth, even at Paul's urging, until they had healed their foolish dispute as to whether he or Paul were the greater.[6] He traveled in other areas of the

---

[1]Acts 18:18-21.
[2]Acts 18:24-28.
[3]By placing her name first, Luke would seem to indicate that Priscilla took the initiative in this invitation to Apollos and in his instruction.
[4]Acts 18:26.
[5]Acts 18:27—19:1 and I Cor. 3:1-15.
[6]I Cor. 16:12.

45

church under Paul's direction,[1] always with zeal and that remarkable eloquence that made his ministry notable. The effect of the sympathetic and earnest counsel given him by Priscilla and Aquila at the outset of his career abode ever with him. He and the Church as a whole owed this devoted couple a great debt in his training.[2]

Aquila and Priscilla Protect Paul

After the journey through rugged Galatia and Phrygia, Paul came to Ephesus, establishing himself for a ministry of some duration. The young church had prospered under the guidance of Aquila and Priscilla with the help of Apollos and others in Paul's corps of workers. Now he took the leadership, and the church grew rapidly in numbers and influence. Ephesus was the port of Asia Minor most directly opposite Corinth, and a continual procession of ships passed from one to the other. A great overland trade was organized touching the interior of Asia Minor and regions far beyond. As at Corinth, so at Ephesus, the Church of Christ stood at the gateway to a huge area and a multitude of people.

With his peculiar dramatic power, Luke describes the uproar that shook Ephesus when Demetrius, leader of the craft of silversmiths, lodged his complaints against Paul.[3] The apostle's life was saved only by the wise counsel and alert protection of his friends, among whom Aquila and Priscilla are definitely to be numbered. Paul never forgot their solicitude and effective action, possibly even in offering themselves as hostages for him, and on a day he sent greetings to them in these terms:

---

[1]Titus 3:13.

[2]A further possible relationship between these friends is discussed in the chapter "Women and the Text of the Bible."

[3]Acts 19:23—20:1.

> Salute Priscilla and Aquila my fellow-workers in Christ Jesus, who
> for my life laid down their own necks; unto whom not only I give
> thanks, but also all the churches of the Gentiles: and salute the
> church that is in their house.[1]

Little did the Emperor Claudius know that these whom he had despised and banished were to travel the eastern reaches of the Empire, displaced and migrant, yet human and true, being hosts to the ambassadors of God, training the ardent advocates of his Kingdom, making their temporary dwelling a radiant center of love and service, the very heart of the Body of Christ.

MARY AND MARTHA

The home of Martha, Mary, and Lazarus had come to mean much to Jesus. They lived at Bethany, on the eastern slope of a long ridge whose western course was called the Mount of Olives. Jerusalem was not in sight of Bethany, for the village was too far around the thrusting crest of Olivet, where the Jericho Road swung across to begin its descent towards the city. Yet it was less than an hour's walk from the crooked crowded streets close to the Temple. Often on his journeys to Jerusalem, Jesus would stop at this home in Bethany for rest and refreshment after the grueling climb up the road from Jericho. Frequently while at the Holy City the Saviour would again visit these loyal friends. Indeed, a careful reading of the account of what we call Holy Week would suggest that the early nights of that tempestuous week were spent quietly under that hospitable roof.

Luke, John, and Matthew record events occurring there of such character as to indicate a close and cordial friendship between this family and Jesus. So close a mutual understanding could have been built up only after long association.[2] There was the time when Martha, the practical

---

[1] Rom. 16:3-5.
[2] Luke 10:38-42; John 11:1-45; 12:1-8 (Matt. 26:6-13).

worker, seemed disturbed because her sister Mary, the mystic, preferred to entertain the Master rather than assist with the preparations. In longer association with Jesus, Martha was to learn the priceless lesson that the practical can never be fully accomplished unless it is infilled with the spiritual, and that when it is so inspired its practicality becomes of eternal meaning rather than just of the fussy and transient. Likewise, Mary came to see that mystic contemplation is a selfish exercise unless it gives issue into beautiful deeds of sharing.

The Fourth Gospel tells the story of the illness, death, and raising of Lazarus. The sorrow of the sisters was most poignant, and so deeply did it move the Saviour that tears coursed down his cheeks as he entered into their grief. Immortal words were spoken, of infinite worth. They would stand forever for the solace and the deathless hope of all who mourn—whether Lazarus had stepped from his tomb or not. It was to Martha, the practical, that these utterances were addressed—these words of transcendant mystical and spiritual import. Whereupon she made her own pronouncement of complete faith:

> Yea, Lord: I have believed that thou art the Christ, the Son of God, even he that cometh into the world.[1]

Martha then quietly turned back to the house and, finding Mary alone where she sat in dejection, said to her:

> The Master is come, and calleth for thee.[2]

The final scene is of a dinner at Bethany, given to Jesus at the home of Simon the leper, during the last week of the Saviour's life. Martha had superintended its preparation and service. Lazarus sat beside the Saviour, strangely prophetic of the Resurrection, so soon to be accomplished.

[1]John 11:27.
[2]John 11:28 (K.J.V.).

The Twelve were present, and others also. Already the impending tragedy cast its shadow over them. During the course of the meal, Mary took her alabaster cruse of very precious unguents and poured the contents upon the Saviour's head. Martha, the practical, made no protest now, for she knew this to be her sister's gift of supreme devotion. When some of the disciples murmured, as materially-minded men sometimes do when they think of unwise investments for the Kingdom that they might have handled to better advantage, Jesus accepted her act in these remarkable words:

> Why trouble ye the woman? for she hath wrought a good work upon me . . . . . For in that she poured this ointment upon my body, she did it to prepare me for burial. Verily I say unto you, Wheresoever this gospel shall be preached in the whole world, that also which this woman hath done shall be spoken of for a memorial of her.[1]

The beautiful life of this home, its growth in spiritual perception, the evident delight in sharing hospitality with the Saviour, and then the transition into the vital and timeless values whereby every human contact is glorified by the divine Presence, is reverently expressed in this poem by Madeleine Sweeney Miller:

To Martha at Bethany: Spring 33 A.D.

Though menial are her tasks,
　　No menial soul she brings
To their accomplishment;
　　But joy within her sings,
For lo! the Guest who asks
　　Her ministry was taught
How toil with meditation blent
　　May be with visions fraught.
No longer cumbered, she, but thrilled
That his bright face has filled
The gloom of her small dwelling place
Again with his transforming grace.
She little dreams that on that kingly head,
　　Which pensive Mary lavishly annoints,

---

[1]Matt. 26:10-13.

49

While Lazarus ponders how he raised him, dead,
  Will soon be pressed dark Calvary's waiting points.
Oh, come, Lord Jesus, knock again
And say wherever toiling men
And women feel their tasks a weight,
  "My Father worketh even until now,
And I still work beside thee, dawn and late,
  And share with thee the drops upon thy brow."[1]

[1]Quoted, with Mrs. Miller's gracious permission, from her book, *New Testament Women and Problems of Today*, pp. 26, 27. Published by The Methodist Book Concern, 1926, New York.

SUGGESTIONS FOR FURTHER STUDY

1. Read the incident of Rahab and the spies at Jericho (Josh. 2:1-22; 6:22-27). Consider whether her hospitality developed from the level of personal advantage to a range of positive spiritual perception and of moral daring. Note that in Matthew's genealogy of the Saviour (1:5), she is recorded as the mother of Boaz and thus the great-great-grandmother of David. She is also included as a heroine of faith in Heb. 11:31.

2. Read the stories concerning Michal and Abigail whom David married early in his career. References to Michal are I Sam. 18:17-29; 19:8-17; 25:44. In her first devotion to David, she was rather like her brother Jonathan. Later, when the ark was brought to Jerusalem, Michal taunted David for his public religious ecstasy (II Sam. 6:12-23). The incidents concerning Abigail are found in I Sam. 25:2-44; 27:3; 30:1-20; II Sam. 2:1-4; 3:1-4. David's words to Abigail in I Sam. 25:32-35, are the noblest he is reported to have spoken to or about any woman. She strengthened him greatly when he was an outlaw.

3. In the concluding paragraphs of Paul's various letters, note the salutations mentioned as to the women of the churches. List the homes that seem to have been centers of organized church activity. How widespread was the custom of maintaining the church in the homes of people?

4. Read both of Paul's letters to Timothy, and the references to him in Acts. Note carefully the major elements in his character as these may be indicated. Evaluate those that seem to be a definite sharing of the background and training of his home.

5. Draw a simple outline map of the lands of the Bible. Mark those areas and cities that have been mentioned thus

51

far in our study. Keep this map, and enter the location of additional places as they are noted in the succeeding chapters of this text. When the study has been completed, you will have a map showing the widespread location of the places where the women of Scripture lived and exerted their influence.

Chapter Three

Career and Business Women

Sᴇᴠᴇʀᴀʟ ᴡᴏᴍᴇɴ ᴏꜰ Sᴄʀɪᴘᴛᴜʀᴇ met and dealt with certain of the individual problems of career and business. These blazed the trail for us today at a number of important points. Such older sisters have words of wise counsel to utter. Their experiences are well worth our prayerful study.

WOMEN AT WORK

Recently *The New York Times* carried this statement:

> Today nearly a million women in the United States are in business for themselves, according to Census Bureau figures. They are proprietors, managers or officers in 442 of 451 types of jobs classified by the Government . . . . . Four times as many women are setting up their own shops as did in 1930[1].

Because of the unexpected trend in the number of women over forty-five years of age who are gainfully employed, Iphigene Bettman has made a careful study in the form of an article, "A Second Career for the Older Woman."[2] She cites Department of Labor statistics indicating that about ten million women over forty-five are now employed, this being an increase of approximately forty-five per cent in this age group since 1940. A full hundred thousand of them are farm owners and managers. Her concluding paragraph is challenging:

> Changed conditions of family life, both as to living and as to loyalties; simplified housekeeping, the increasing acceptance of all women as wage-earners, the decreasing disapproval of married work-

---

[1]September 23, 1948. Used by permission.
[2]*The New York Times Magazine*, October 10, 1948, pp. 22-28. Used by permission.

53

ers, better health, increasing longevity—all these contribute to a fresh outlook for the woman past forty-five. When the load of family is lifted, she retains too much vitality to be discarded. A new type of American woman, the older paid worker and business woman, is apparently in the making.

The doors to a multitude of activities stand open for the woman of today. Though we readily accept this fact for our own land, we may be surprised at the way it holds true over the world. In the official labor statistics of America, approximately seven hundred distinct types of gainful employment are listed. Of these considerably less than fifty are still exclusively occupied by men.[1] All other types are available to women, and a tentative approach is being made by occasional individuals to some of the occupations that have been looked upon hitherto as solely masculine.

Women in Leadership

Increasing numbers of women are moving from the ranks of the employed to the categories of employer, executive, or professional career person. In art, music, literature, education, medicine, the law, gifted women have long since found their fields for appropriate life-career. The numbers of these are now multiplied as educational opportunities have developed, and the newer facilities for the home have given greater personal leisure to many. The total of women to be included in the professional career group will doubtless steadily grow, and their privileges of distinguished humanitarian service and vital public leadership will be correspondingly enhanced. In the business world a host of women occupy posts of executive responsibility. This is notably true in banking, insurance, journalism, merchandising, light manufactures, publications, social welfare

---

[1] The so-called "heavy-muscled" series, such as sandhogs, steeplejacks, steel-riveters, deep-sea divers; the combat elements of the armed forces; in professional athletics, the physical contact-group, baseball, football, wrestling, and pugilism.

and relief administration. Almost unlimited possibilities lie in these fields for women of adequate training and resilient personality.

Problems of Adjustment

Many problems, some quite serious and intricate, are created by the increasing entry of women into the world of the shop, factory, business office, laboratory. Some of the questions are broadly social in character, and must find their answer on the level of the community and nation as a whole. Some are distinctly personal, and show the infinite variations of unrepeating individuality. These have to do with adjustments in the life of the home, among the members of the family circle. Often they involve intimate obligations regarding which the person may not have much choice other than accept the duty and carry it, as far as may be possible, to final accomplishment.

Naturally, within the scope and purpose of this study, it cannot be ours to present the detail of the sociological factors. The warm and delicate personal problem frequently needs wise and careful guidance. Only occasionally can its solution be found already set forth in the cold analysis of the printed page. The human example, the vivid experience of others, is often the best guide.

MIRIAM, SISTER OF MOSES

The most commonly known incidents of Miriam's life are those connected with the finding of her baby brother, Moses, by Egypt's princess at the shore of the Nile.[1] Without the clever assistance of her young daughter, Jochebed might have been quite unable to save her tiny son in the way she did, thus assuring him the opportune destiny that

[1]Exod. 2:1-10.

seemed to be appointed for him of God. However, Miriam's highest privilege, years later, was to co-operate with Moses in his own supreme achievement, a fact that is more frequently overlooked than recognized.

In the appropriate section of our first chapter, we looked into the home of Amram and Jochebed, estimating as best we could the sort of training the devoted mother gave to her three talented children.[1] Miriam evidently possessed certain marked traits of personality that conspired to set her apart among her people. She remained unmarried, which fact under ordinary circumstances in that day would have relegated her to complete obscurity. Nonetheless, her natural graces—a quick understanding of the problems of her sex in slavery, a gift for poetry and melody, and a burning zeal for the God of her fathers (she herself being of Levite parentage)—gave her quite early in life a place of unique leadership among the Hebrew women.[2] The fact that she did not have intimate family obligations of her own made it possible for her to assume such a position of authority as is indicated. She held close and continuous relationship with her brother Aaron, and at times strongly influenced his thinking and action.[3]

Her Co-operation With Moses

The record of the appearances of Moses and Aaron before Pharaoh Merenptah,[4] and of the attendant events concluding with the escape of the Hebrew people and the great loss

[1]This section should be re-read with special attention to the references to Miriam.

[2]There is no written record of these characteristics of Miriam, for the historians were interested more directly in showing the work of Moses. The inferences are, however, fully justified in the light of such notations concerning her as do appear.

[3]Notably in their joint criticism of Moses in the desert, Num. 12:1-16, to which reference is made in a subsequent paragraph.

[4]He succeeded Rameses II upon his death, c. 1225-1215 B. C., Exod. 2:23.

suffered by the Egyptian army, comprises one of the most dramatic sections of all Scripture.[1] Herein the freedom of the Hebrews from slavery was achieved, and the process of welding them into a nation was begun.

At the crossing of the Bitter Lakes,[2] Miriam's qualities were amply demonstrated. Her grip on the situation held the women and their small children under control. They crossed over in good order, and without panic, despite the terrifying charge of the Egyptian chariots and cavalry. With the escape from Egypt accomplished, Miriam stood before the women, gathered on the far bank of the lakes, leading them in her own stirring antiphonal paean of victory whose refrain was:

> Sing ye to Jehovah for he hath triumphed gloriously:
> The horse and his rider hath he thrown into the sea.[3]

Miriam proved herself an effective lieutenant to Moses, and the willingness to follow him into the desert, bravely evidenced by the household groups on more than one occasion, was doubtless the result of her loyal and brilliant leadership. The later historian, writing of the events at the Red Sea, called her "the prophetess,"[4] she being the first among the very few Hebrew women to whom this astonishing title was given.

Her Sin and Its Pardon

Long months later in the desert, she unwisely allowed a rankling personal bitterness to drive her from the place of loyalty to Moses into a public criticism of his method and a challenge as to whether God spoke more directly through

---

[1]Exodus 5 through 13.
[2]The modern name of the location to which the Red Sea then extended.
[3]Exod. 15:21. Verses 1—17 of this chapter constitute a song of high poetic order, one of the most notable in the Old Testament. It is discussed in the chapter "Women and the Text of the Bible."
[4]Exod. 15:20.

him or through her.[1] Aaron was enough under her influence to stand with her. For this public affront to Moses, God smote her with dread leprosy.[2] Moses, who might well have shown anger and resentment against them both, held himself in check. His simple and sincere prayer before all the people for her forgiveness and healing[3] brought her restoration (albeit the people could not move forward from that place for seven days, until the ritual for the expiation of her uncleanness from leprosy was accomplished).[4]

With Jehovah's pardon made effective in the disappearance of her leprosy, she evidently resumed her accustomed place with the women, judging among them on Moses' behalf, inspiring them in face of continuing hardship. The shock of her tragic mistake and bitter experience took its toll, however, as she was approaching the advanced years of her life. It was not long before her death, at Kadesh in the wilderness of Zin.[5] Josephus, the noted Jewish historian, declares that thirty full days were then devoted to public mourning for her, and that the day of her death was memorialized for centuries. So great had been her influence, and for so long had its potent meaning been regarded, that the prophet Micah, eager contemporary of Isaiah, called it to witness as an enduring testimony to the goodness of God even unto his own backsliding generation:

> O my people, what have I done unto thee? and wherein have I wearied thee? testify against me. For I brought thee up out of the land of Egypt, and redeemed thee out of the house of bondage; and I sent before thee Moses, Aaron and Miriam.[6]

Her Career of Selfless Service

Miriam heads the roll of a multitude of devout women who, from her distant day to ours, have given themselves in glad

[1]Num. 12:1-15.   [4]Num. 12:15.
[2]See also Deut. 24:9.   [5]Num. 20:1.
[3]Num. 12:13.   [6]Mic. 6:3, 4.

devotion to the service of those less fortunate. In the earlier epochs very few women could find the natural freedom of action for such a career. Every social custom and usage was set rigidly against them. By some peculiar grace Miriam managed to shatter the walls that would have confined her. Deborah, a century or so later, also wrought the miracle of a great career, at another angle of life.[1] But before the dawn of the Christian era there were only a very few such heroines.

The freedom of thought, status, and action that has come to women of all races across the world, as the Saviour's regal gift, is beyond words adequately to estimate. What Paul calls "the glorious liberty of the children of God"[2] has this as one of its chief factors. In his letter to the churches of Galatia he sets in startling phrases the basic contrasts between the confining limits of the old way of life and the indescribable freedom that comes in Christ:

> For ye are all sons of God, through faith, in Christ Jesus. For as many of you as were baptized into Christ did put on Christ. There can be neither Jew nor Greek, there can be neither bond nor free, there can be no male and female; for ye are all one man in Christ Jesus.[3]

One of Britain's most eminent missionaries in China has put it in this fashion:

> When we truly read, learn, mark and digest the Gospels, ... we find that every one of woman's experiences mattered to Jesus Christ, and at every stage of her life—in health and in sickness, as she lived alongside other women, as well as when in the company of husband and children. Jesus never ignored her sex, or her femininity, but neither did He think of her only or chiefly because of it. To Him she was a human being, and His Father was her Father, as He told Mary Magdalene in the garden.[4]

A great company of women today walk this road of

[1]The work of Deborah is discussed in the following section.
[2]Rom. 8:21 (K. J. V.).
[3]Gal. 3:26-28.
[4]Lady Hosie, *Jesus and Woman* (London: Hodder & Stoughton, Ltd., 1946), p. 19. A very important book—to be studied carefully, if at all accessible.

glorious service that was marked out and pioneered by
Miriam and those who followed her

> . . . . Prepare ye in the wilderness the way of Jehovah; make level
> in the desert a highway for our God. Every valley shall be exalted,
> and every mountain and hill shall be made low; and the uneven
> shall be made level, and the rough places a plain: and the glory of
> Jehovah shall be revealed, and all flesh shall see it together . . . . [1]

DEBORAH, THE PROPHETESS

As Miriam was the first, so Deborah was the second woman
in Scripture to be known by the very unusual title of prophetess.[2] Apparantly soon after the death of Joshua, Deborah came into prominence as a judge before the people.
She established her seat somewhere "between Ramah and
Beth-el in the hill-country of Ephraim."[3] Indeed this
location was so close to Timnath-serah where Joshua was
buried,[4] and the time of her public appearance so soon
after his death,[5] that she must be thought of as having
assumed leadership almost directly after him. In her
younger years she had doubtless seen Joshua frequently, and
her training had evidently come from those who had known
him intimately, skilled in the laws and the methods he had
learned from Moses.

Deborah was thus trained and equipped to carry forward
the worship of Jehovah and the instruction and inspiration
of the people in his law. So potent did her influence become,
that the great palm tree under which she was accustomed
to sit in official capacity was popularly called by her very
name. It is recorded that "the children of Israel came up

---

[1]Isa. 40:3-5.

[2]Judg. 4:4. Her parents' names are not recorded. Lapidoth was her
husband. There is no record of their family, if any.

[3]Judg. 4:5. Eight to ten miles north of Jerusalem, which was still, however, in Canaanite hands.

[4]Josh. 24:29-31 (Judg. 2:6-10).

[5]The battle with Sisera, the climax of her career (c. 1150 B.C.), occurred
not much more than 50 years after Joshua captured Jericho.

to her for judgment."[1] They found in her the consolation they needed in trial, wise counsel in practical affairs, a hatred and contempt for the petty and vile, strong confidence in the future—all based on a profound and unshaken faith in God and in his constant love and care for those who trusted in him. The fire of virile faith and the glory of noble conduct were magnetic forces that drew the people from year to year to the palm tree of Deborah near Beth-el in Ephraim.

It was an appallingly cruel and turbulent age. The Hebrew tribes, with unequal success, had attempted the subjugation of the various sections of the land allotted to them. However, a line of powerful Canaanite cities westward from Jerusalem to the coast held out stubbornly. The southern edge of the great Plain of Esdraelon boasted another series of strongly fortified bastions that remained uncaptured—Harosheth near the Mediterranean, Megiddo,[2] Taanach, Jenin, Jezreel, Bethshean. The wide and fertile area of the plain was under Canaanite control. Along the southern section of the Mediterranean coast the piratical Philistines were rapidly gaining the ascendancy with their practical monopoly in iron for tools and weapons of all sorts.[3] From east of the Jordan hordes of raiding Midianites and related tribes frequently assailed the land. They warred against one another—Canaanite, Hebrew, Philistine, Midianite—across the two centuries of fire, blood, pillage and rapine, from the fall of Jericho under Joshua to the death of King Saul.[4]

---

[1] Judg. 4:5.
[2] From this name the word Armageddon is derived.
[3] I Sam. 13:19-23.
[4] The Books of Joshua, Judges, Ruth, and I Samuel should be read consecutively with careful notation of the rapidly changing political situation and the harsh and cruel social order. Each book, except Ruth, would require about two hours of thoughtful study. The time and effort would be well repaid in the finer appreciation gained of the life and work of such women as Rahab, Deborah, Naomi, Ruth, Hannah, David's mother, Abigail, Michal.

Her Aid to Barak

During the years of Deborah's developing influence a
sinister force had been growing in power in the north. The
Canaanite king Jabin, ruling from Hazor between Mt.
Tabor and Lake Huleh, was in process of securing complete
control from the hills of Samaria northward.[1] Sisera of
Harosheth was his chief captain and charioteer. With the
strength of their fortified positions along the rim of
Esdraelon and the mobile striking force of several hundred
chariots, they kept the Hebrews to the hills and harried
them in every possible way. The communications among
the Hebrews from settlement to settlement were cut; their
crops and caravans were ravaged; their very villages were
looted and destroyed.[2]

After the agony of long months of quiet suffering and of
urgent prayer for her people, the word of Jehovah came to
Deborah. Under its impact she threw aside the cloak of
peace and took the sword and shield. As she herself sang
about it in her incomparable paean of triumph, all these
woes occurred

> Until that I Deborah arose,
> That I arose a mother in [for] Israel.[3]

Barak of Kadesh-naphtali was the most likely leader
for such a host as might be summoned.[4] His village was
perched high in the hills above Jabin's fortresses. He knew
the disposition of Sisera's chariot-groups, as well as every
obscure trail the Hebrews must use to effect their swift and
secret mobilization. Deborah called him to the attack with

---

[1] Judg. 4:1-3.
[2] Note the stanzas in Deborah's battle song (Judg. 5:6, marginal readings):
"The caravans ceased . . . . travellers walked through crooked ways. The
villages were unoccupied . . . . ."
[3] Judg. 5:7.
[4] His name means "lightning," "thunderbolt."

a definite word of victory from Jehovah.[1] Yet even Barak would not make the venture unless Jehovah's prophetess Deborah was in the forefront, for only thus could he feel sure of Jehovah's favor and of his presence for the promised victory.

> And Barak said unto her, If thou wilt go with me, then I will go; but if thou wilt not go with me, I will not go. And she said, I will surely go with thee: notwithstanding, the journey that thou takest shall not be for thine honor; for Jehovah will sell Sisera into the hand of a woman . . . . .[2]

With the assurance of Deborah's presence, Barak blew the trumpet for the tribes. Naphtali and Zebulon answered immediately. Deborah brought strong contingents from Ephraim and Benjamin. The Hebrews gathered on the slopes of Mt. Tabor, which rose as a great dome above the plain, looking down upon all the roads along which Sisera's chariots must come from their various stations from Harosheth to Bethshean.

Thus the strategy was set for battle, when into it Jehovah seemed to make catastrophic entry in one of the wild, rolling thunder-storms with a veritable cloudburst such as occasionally sweep the plain. The lush fields became quagmires. The brook Kishon, usually a mere trickle and often entirely dry, was suddenly turned into a raging torrent overrushing every bank and flooding wide areas as the encircling hills, north and south, fed their heavy drainage of the storm. Groups of chariots were caught in flank and rear. Others were quickly isolated. They could not turn into position for the invincible charge wheel to wheel. Cloying mud held them. Horses floundered, slipped, and fell. And from every side the agile footmen of Barak swarmed amongst them until the vaunted chariot-force of Sisera was

---

[1]Judg. 4:6, 7.
[2]Judg. 4:8, 9. Jael, the wife of Heber the Kenite, slew Sisera in flight after his defeat by Barak (Judg. 4:17-22).

annihilated. After the battle, Deborah sang of it thus:

> The earth trembled, the heavens also dropped,
> Yea, the clouds dropped water.
> The mountains quaked at the presence of Jehovah,
>
> . . . .
>
> Then fought the kings of Canaan,
> In Taanach by the water of Megiddo:
>
> . . . .
>
> From heaven fought the stars,
> From their courses they fought against Sisera.
> The river Kishon swept them away,
> That ancient river, the river Kishon.
>
> . . . .
>
> Then did the horsehoofs stamp
> By reason of the prancings, the prancings of their strong ones.[1]

The decimation of his army broke Jabin's power. Archaeological evidence shows that within a very short time after this battle Megiddo was captured by the Hebrews and became one of their new outposts.[2]

> And the hand of the children of Israel prevailed more and more against Jabin the king of Canaan, until they had destroyed Jabin king of Canaan.[3]

This victory of Deborah and Barak climaxed the conquest of Palestine.[4] From then on the Canaanites were under control. Defense was still necessary against enemies from without—Midianites, Philistines, and others—but the basis for interior security and unity was laid. Tremendous as this achievement appears in the defeat of Sisera, it must

---

[1]Judg. 5:4, 5, 19-22. The entire chapter comprises Deborah's song of triumph.

[2]See EBL, p. 265, and illustrations 47 and 156, for description and pictures of jewelry found in Megiddo excavations covering the period of capture by the Hebrews. At a later date Solomon made Megiddo and Jabin's Hazor to be twin pivots for his system of northern defense (I Kings 9:15). The writer has visited the excavations on this historic site seeing the stone posts in Solomon's chariot stables, thrusting fingers into the very holes through which the halter ropes for the horses were passed.

[3]Judg. 4:24.

[4]The exploit was of sufficient significance to win for Barak a niche in Faith's Hall of Fame (Heb. 11:32).

never be forgotten that it was made possible only as based on the long years of faithful and virtuous leadership evidenced by Deborah in her peaceful role as judge and prophetess.

She holds an utterly unique place among the women of the Old Testament, for she is the only one of whom it is recorded that she guided them in both moral and spiritual judgment, and also led them to martial victory in the day of great crisis. Yet, she could not have succeeded save for the devotion of countless other unnamed women who found inspiration in her leadership and for the loyalty whereby they sent forth their men for the battle. The consecrated and God-fearing women who hold places of influence in public affairs today count greatly on the continuing prayer and the sympathetic understanding of the multitude of women in the churches.

LYDIA, CHRISTIAN BUSINESS WOMAN

Lydia was in business at Philippi when Paul came to that city in the year 53 A.D. Luke, Silas, and Timothy were his companions. Writing about this journey at a later date, Luke speaks of Lydia as "a seller of purple, of the city of Thyatira."[1] This probably means that she was an agent for the importing and selling of the famous dyed fabrics of Asia Minor. She was accordingly a person of influence in the business and social life of the noted city.

The City in Which Lydia Lived

Luke describes Paul's voyage as from Troas,[2] close to the site of Troy, famed in Homer's epic poem of the ancient Greeks. Their ship stopped at the island of Samothrace over

[1]Acts 16:14.
[2]Acts 16:11.

night. There they must have seen the perfect statue we know as the "Winged Victory of Samothrace."[1] She stood on the prow of a stone ship set on the edge of a cliff overlooking the harbor. Close to her a great fire-beacon was burned every night as a guide to mariners. Paul's ship sailed next day for Neapolis,[2] port of Philippi, just as Piraeus is the port of Athens; but he never forgot this vision of victory.

When Paul and his friends reached Philippi, they found a city very proud of its history. Three hundred years earlier, Philip of Macedon had made it great when he chose it for the new capital of his kingdom, and gave it his name. He completely rebuilt the place, erecting notable public buildings, graceful temples, and commodious wharves at Neapolis. He lavished much of the gold upon it that he mined at near-by Mt. Pangaeus.

At Philippi, the city in which Lydia lived, Alexander, Philip's son, grew to manhood, dreaming of the world empire that might be his some day. The stud-like islands of the blue Aegean Sea that he glimpsed from the crest of Pangaeus seemed ever to beckon him. When Alexander was but twenty, an assassin took Philip's life. Immediately Alexander marched forth to take the world. His queen-mother held Philippi firmly for him, with the limitless wealth of his Pangaean mines at his disposal. With amazing skill Alexander hurled his undefeated phalanxes across the continents until he ruled from the Black Sea to the Nile, from the shores of the Adriatic to the rivers of India. And Philippi was the settled capital from which he had set forth, and to which he hoped to return.

Proud as Philippi's citizens were of her ancient fame, Paul

---

[1] For years this glorious statue has been one of the chief attractions at the Louvre in Paris.
[2] Meaning "new city."

found them most keenly conscious of their present glory. A scant century before (B.C. 42), the army of Antony and Octavian had routed the forces of Brutus and Cassius at the very gates of the city. In this terrific battle both Brutus and Cassius died.[1] Ten years later, a decisive naval engagement, fought on the Aegean within full view of Philippi, was won by Octavian over Antony and Cleopatra. On these victories Octavian, soon to be called Augustus, had founded the Roman Empire.[2]

As reward, the veterans of these campaigns had been settled in Philippi with inalienable Roman citizenship bestowed upon them and their sons. Philippi was declared a Roman colony of the first rank,[3] with the very laws of Rome itself as its inviolable privilege. Thus it was that these laws were invoked by some at Philippi when they disliked Paul's preaching of Christ:

> . . . . These men, being Jews, do exceedingly trouble our city, and set forth customs which it is not lawful for us to receive, or to observe, being Romans.[4]

Lydia, Agent at Philippi

To Philippi, Roman colony of the first rank, site of the decisive battles that had forged the Empire, the woman, Lydia, had come from Thyatira. She was to be agent at Philippi for the weaving and dyeing industry of her home province. So closely allied was she with her old environment, that her personal name was actually that of her province—Lydia.

For generations the Lydian market, as it was called, had

---

[1]Shakespeare dramatized the epic event in the last act of *Julius Caesar*.
[2]Read the pertinent chapter in Will Durant's *Caesar and Christ* (New York: Simon & Schuster, 1944), pp. 206, 207, 219.
[3]Acts 16:12.
[4]Acts 16:20,21.

enjoyed a wide and very valuable trade throughout the Graeco-Roman world. Among the products of the province were objects of bronze wrought into fascinating designs, and rugs, and a certain type of exquisite jewelry. But above all else, Lydia was famous for its textiles—marvelous linens and fine cotton materials, either plain or beautifully dyed. The famous dyes were of two kinds. One was a vegetable type, extracted from the madder, a plant that grew luxuriantly in every river valley. The other was taken from the murex, a mollusk that flourished in vast beds in the shoals along the seacoast. Indeed, the profitable murex was gathered as far south as Tyre, just above the border of Palestine. These dyes ranged from a brilliant crimson to a dark, lustrous purple. The actual Greek word which we translate "purple" had become the popular trade-name for the entire Lydian industry of dyed textiles.

The province Lydia had five large cities.[1] Two were on the coast—Ephesus and Smyrna. They possessed extensive textile and dyeing factories, and good harbors with excellent shipping facilities. Three cities were inland centers for the Lydian products—Sardis, Philadelphia, Thyatira—located on the chief rivers and connected with the coastal cities by good roads. From Thyatira, center of weaving of the finest linen, the woman, Lydia, had gone to Philippi to be agent there for the textiles (purple) of the Lydian market. As a Roman colony of the first rank, and from its historical setting, Philippi was important enough in its own right. But with the vantage point as a harbor given it by Philip and developed by the Romans, it had become noteworthy as the entry-port for a huge hinterland. Roads and caravan routes radiated from Philippi to

[1]These five cities are mentioned frequently in the New Testament, Ephesus being supremely important.

the Black Sea, the plains of southeastern Europe, and around the head of the Adriatic to northern Italy and on to Rome itself.

The beautiful products of the looms of Thyatira and of the entire dyeing industry, were in great demand. Bolts of the finest material brought incredible prices. Wealthy Greek and Roman ladies vied in displaying garments of the newest Lydian fabric and design. The agent for the purple at Philippi must be a person of charming social grace, as well as of accredited business ability. This was Lydia of Thyatira when Paul came to Philippi in the year 53.

Lydia, the Christian Hostess

At Troas, Paul had been impelled to Philippi by the vision of the man from Macedonia who implored him, "Come over into Macedonia, and help us."[1] Straightway he undertook the voyage with Luke, Silas, and Timothy as his companions. Arriving at some new place, Paul always promptly made contact with such groups of God-fearing people as could be found. Frequently these worshiped in a synagogue.[2] Occasionally, as at Philippi, they were wont to gather, not in a building, but at some quiet and undisturbed spot of natural beauty.

> And on the sabbath day we went orth without the gate by a river side, where we supposed there was a place of prayer; and we sat down, and spake unto the women that were come together.[3]

Among those who frequented this place of worship was Lydia of Thyatira. Paul's words and exhortation found ready response in her mind and heart. After a period of devotion and training, she was baptized with her family and retinue. Luke writes:

[1]Acts 16:9.
[2]Acts 13:5; 13:14; 14:1; 17:1-4; 18:4.
[3]Acts 16:13.

> And when she was baptized, and her household, she besought us, saying, If ye have judged me to be faithful to the Lord, come into my house, and abide there. And she constrained us.[1]

Paul and his friends lodged thus in the household of Lydia until the riot was set against him over the incident of the healing of the demoniac girl.[2] Imprisonment and cruel scourging followed immediately for Paul and Silas. Then came the sudden earthquake and the conversion of the jailor. When the magistrates learned of the Roman citizenship of Paul and Silas, they were greatly disturbed. The very laws of Rome, which were their glorious heritage, had been broken in Philippi by the scourging of these uncondemned Roman citizens. The magistrates would have dismissed Paul privately, lest there be further unseemly public demonstrations. But Paul demanded:

> They have beaten us publicly, uncondemned, men that are Romans, and have cast us into prison; and do they now cast us out privily? nay, verily; but let them come themselves and bring us out.[3]

At this, the magistrates came and ushered them out of the prison. Leaving the prison and magistrates, Paul and Silas

> . . . . entered into the house of Lydia: and when they had seen the brethren, they comforted them, and departed.[4]

Luke and Timothy remained in Philippi to shepherd this first church formally established on the continent of Europe, meeting at the home of Lydia, Christian business woman.

When Paul came to Philippi in the year 53, it was as the ambassador of God's world-wide and eternal Kingdom entering the capital of one past great kingdom, and the actual foundation place of the empire that then controlled the known world. Here, this ambassador of Christ established a church that was to live closer to his own heart than any other of all those he was to know. There is a warm and

---

[1]Acts 16:15.
[2]Acts 16:16.
[3]Acts 16:37.
[4]Acts 16:40.

intimate love in his epistle to the Philippians, written a decade later when he was himself a prisoner in Rome, not found in any other of his letters. It was Paul's personal pride to support himself and his companions with the labor of his hands as a skilled maker of tent-cloth. The record indicates that of all the churches, he permitted only the Philippians to contribute to his own necessity, and that more than once.[1]

When Lydia came to Philippi, she was to be the manager of the growing enterprise of her native province. Yet, it was also in her house that this ambassador of Christ was to dwell. It was from her house that he was to leave, recognized publicly as an honored citizen of Rome. To her house the Church of God was to come for worship and comfort, as Luke and Timothy guided its growth from the gracious circle of her influence. And on a day, Paul was to write to these dear friends of the church, originally centering in her home, conscious with proud dignity of their Roman citizenship,

. . . . we are a colony of Heaven, ...[2]

The home of Lydia, the Christian business woman, thus became the first embassy of the kingdom of God in Europe, located at Philippi, Roman colony of the first rank.

PHOEBE AT CENCHREAE

I commend unto you Phoebe our sister, who is a servant of the church that is at Cenchreae: that ye receive her in the Lord, worthily of the saints, and that ye assist her in whatsoever matter she may have need of you: for she herself also hath been a helper of many, and of mine own self.[3]

In this short paragraph Paul introduced Phoebe, deaconess of the church at Cenchreae, to the great church in Ephesus.

[1]Phil. 4:10-20.
[2]Phil. 3:20 James Moffatt, *A New Translation of the New Testament* (New York: Harper & Brothers, 1935). Used by permission.
[3]Rom. 16:1,2.

It is practically agreed among scholars that the chapter from which this statement is taken (Romans 16) is in reality a brief salutation addressed to the church in Ephesus, rather than a sort of postscript to the lengthy letter to Rome. The letter to the church at Rome comes to a thoroughly satisfactory ending with the fifteenth chapter. Most of the people mentioned in this additional section are known to have belonged to the Ephesian church. In the setting up of some very early manuscript there evidently was room for this short, personal letter in the space remaining after the copying of *Romans* had been completed. This letter was then included in the scroll, and later scribes called it "Romans 16" when the division into chapters and verses was instituted.

This is the only reference to Phoebe, but it is sufficient to indicate that she was a woman of definite personality and genuine responsibility in position and influence. Cenchreae was the eastern port section of Corinth, fronting on the Aegean Sea, facing towards Asia. The church at Corinth had developed sufficiently to warrant the establishing of a separate congregation in Cenchreae. Phoebe was deaconess in this church, the word translated "servant" being the technical word for "deaconess."[1] The duties of this office are expounded in Paul's various letters. They involve ministry to the sick, the impoverished, the widows; instruction of children; general services of the church. Informal ordination appears to have been practiced in designation to that office. Blameless life, depth of consecration, unusual training in the Scriptures, ability to serve all without distinction of persons, a certain gift of public speech, were apparently necessary requirements. This was Phoebe's honored status in the church.

---

[1]"Deaconess" is the marginal reading.

In the last clause of this commendation Paul declared her to have been "a helper of many, and of mine own self." The Greek word *prostatis*, translated "helper," was a term of definite technical meaning in the business and legal practice of the time. Frequently persons, by reason of legal status, were disqualified from appearance in a court of law, or from the privilege of signing a contract, or of buying or selling property or goods. Again, in the absence of a properly qualified person, these functions might be required on his behalf. A *prostatis* could perform the necessary service. The function combined some aspects of a modern "agent," or of a person equipped with another's power of attorney. To act as *prostatis* for another, one must hold his own proper legal status, be possessed of resources, be able to make a formal public address, be acquainted with the many forms of business and legal procedure.

Phoebe was evidently such a person, qualified to practice in the Corinth area. Business for some one took her to Ephesus. Paul gave her this charming letter of cordial endorsement to the Christian fellowship, and a score of rich personal contacts were opened at once to her by the intimate greetings included in the document. Godliness of spirit, loving service to those in need, the honor of the Church, lived in the soul of this deaconess, whose acute mind, tireless efforts, and real integrity held important responsibilities for the business and legal problems of others, including the apostle himself. Many capable women of today hold membership in the guild of noble servants of the church, custodians of the property and well-being of others, founded by Phoebe of Cenchreae.

The deaconesses of Methodism hold an honored place in the organization and economy of the church. Opportunities for them in varied fields of service under The Methodist

Church are almost unlimited. A deaconess may serve as a teacher or a college president; as a nurse or a hospital chaplain—a number of our important hospitals are largely staffed by deaconesses; as a teacher or director of religious education; as a pastor or pastor's assistant; as a national or conference director of children's and youth work; as a student counselor or a Wesley Foundation worker; as a specialist in one of many phases of social work in a rural community or in a city settlement. Wherever they serve, the consecration and grace of deaconesses aid profoundly in the care of the suffering and in helpful visitation in homes of need and distress. These trained and consecrated women stand in the direct line of succession of Phoebe, deaconess of the noted church of Cenchreae.

THE CHALLENGE TO CHRISTIAN BUSINESS WOMEN

The church is keenly interested in its countless employed women. The thousand intimate personal problems they face may open ways by which the grace of God and the indwelling guidance of his Spirit may more completely permeate life. If adjustments in the organization and the life of the home are effected, the glory of God may dwell there in richer measure than ever before experienced. If the test is in co-operation and teamwork with others, and at the same time in holding true to vital faith and moral conviction, great opportunities for spiritual achievement are present. The thrusting of thousands of eager Christian women into the intricacies and structure of the working world constitutes an open door of wide dimension for the entry of Christian influence and power.

The four women of the Bible whose experiences in public life we have studied lived in differing ages and cultures.

Their specialized spheres were quite distinct one from another. Yet they solved their problems and made a tremendous contribution to their situations, and to us today, by their constancy in one abiding principle for glorious, successful living. They were, above all else, vividly and thrillingly aware of God. They translated that abiding sense of his presence into the practical business of every day and the total meaning of life. This gave them conquering power over evil. It made them proof against the subtle atmosphere of paganism that pervaded so much of the culture in their epochs. They were God's women, and he ever lived in their hearts.

The life of our present world faces saturation by the deadly poison of secularism, which is a day-by-day thoroughgoing atheism.

> It has become the supporting atmosphere of our culture. To describe it is like describing the air about us. No logical knife can dissect it; it is too pervasive and fluid to be captured in the net of any system of ideas. We are so completely adjusted to it that we do not mark it, but only those salient parts of our culture for which it is the permanent foundation . . . . . Secularism is our failure to let God be God in our lives. Its nature is neither to affirm nor to deny religious faith, but to live indifferently to it. Neither reverence nor blasphemy does it know. Saint and devil alike are no secularists, for both fear God, though one rejoices and the other trembles.[1]

These women of ours, multiplied thousands of them, from our Christian homes and active in the Church of Christ, hold tryst with destiny as they move in and out of the world of business, industry, and the professions. Will they maintain, pulsing and alive, their consciousness of God? Will they strive ever to walk at his side, knowing that as they do this he will ever ward over them wherever they may be called upon to go? Will they know resurgent

---

[1]Leroy E. Leomker, in "The Nature of Secularism," first paper in *The Christian Faith and Secularism*, Abingdon-Cokesbury Press, p. 11. Quoted by permission. A volume of great value to the serious student of present-day religious problems.

within them his grace, sufficient for every need—his strength, whereby they can do all things? Will they be able, each in her own place of vital relationships and of kindling influence, to make his presence real, even beyond themselves, bringing cleansing to life, redeeming it?

Midway in Gounod's opera "Faust," Valentine comes upon the crowd, bemused by the magic of Mephistopheles, dancing in the pagan circle about him as he sings the ballad of "The Calf of Gold." Shocked to his soul, Valentine challenges the incarnation of Evil. In the first pass, Satan exultingly shatters Valentine's sword almost to the hilt. Only a few inches of jagged blade remain. Grasping the broken rapier, even though its edge cut him deep, Valentine thrusts the cross-shaped hilt at Satan, who turns in terror to flee as Valentine sings:

> "C'est une Croix
> Qui de l'Enfer nous garde!"[1]

METHODIST WOMEN AT WORK

The Methodist Church treasures its women who hold place in this strategic area of life. Some occupy posts of very great importance in national and international affairs. Many are responsible for issues in business, or the professions, or the creative achievements of art and literature. A multitude build ceaselessly in the growing structure of the kingdom of God among all sorts of people.

In the organized life and service of The Methodist Church, the Woman's Society of Christian Service is set apart for this aspect of work. Notable leadership is given, high ideals inculcated, selfless service promoted. Within this organization the Wesleyan Service Guild is established primarily to meet the needs and develop the interests of the

---

[1] "It is a Cross that defends us against Hell!"

employed woman. This group is always a potent factor in the local congregation, and its influence and opportunities increase with the days. Not only does it afford a means for skilled employed women to co-operate effectively in the life and work of the church; it offers that organic relationship whereby they may strengthen, undergird, guide and inspire each other on the basis of their unique experiences and common objectives. In addition, the Guild provides the channel through which the skills and techniques, acquired by this group, may flow into the life and work of the church as a single and powerful current.

The writer holds great appreciation for such a group in a certain church of which he was once pastor. Organized a number of years before the merger of the three denominations, it was in its area a forerunner of the Wesleyan Service Guild. Principles and teachers, nurses and social workers, artists and musicians, business executives and secretarial personnel, co-operated in a program of devotion, service, study, and practical work that profoundly influenced the total church. This very group of women, still vitally active, has organized a second guild, for women in their twenties, whose eager work and spiritual resources are already effective in the church.

Further, The Methodist Church is proud to recognize her employed women in official designation and wide responsibility in the corporate life of the church. There is an increasing number of local official boards using the able and effective membership of women of the congregation. Very many boards of trustees and managers, from local churches to universities, include women of ability and acumen in their posts of corporate, legal, and financial obligation. A poll of the women who are active lay delegates in the Annual Conferences would demonstrate their participation in this fundamental duty of the life of the denomination. In the Jurisdictional Conferences, the Central Conferences overseas, and ultimately in the General Conference, the presence and active work of the women elected to those responsibilities carry this tradition and practice into the ultimate legislative groups of the church. It is distinctly in point to note that in the 1948 General Conference, meeting in Boston, one out of every six of the Annual Conferences represented had elected a woman as the leader of the lay delegation of that conference.[1]

Back of those in posts of leadership and high duty, stand the multiplied thousands of women. Whether active primarily in the home, or in industry, or in business, or in the professions, these women of the Church strive, first of all, to be disciples of Christ. Their liberties come from his pierced hand. Their hearts are cleansed by his precious blood. Their lives are inspired by his eternal Spirit of love and service. The world is to be won for him. By faith in him, with loyalty to the church, transforming each service into a holy ministry, and accepting the mission for themselves, they follow him to the ends of the earth, and deep into the heart of humanity's great need.

---

[1] Of the 138 Annual Conferences, exactly one-sixth, 23, had women as the first lay delegate. Of these 23, four were from overseas—Europe, India, the Philippines.

SUGGESTIONS FOR FURTHER STUDY

1. Read the passages that describe the career of Jezebel (I Kings 16:29—19:21; 21:29; II Kings 9:1-37). She took her business as queen most seriously and was an ardent devotee of her god, Melkart, Baal of Tyre. She was a woman of boundless energy and intense singleness of purpose. Consider what might have been achieved had her devotion been for the righteousness of Jehovah. Wherein is this a parable for the day in which we live?

2. In I Kings 18:41-46, note the other great storm that covered the Plain of Esdraelon, and how Elijah ran before King Ahab's chariot all the way from Mt. Carmel to Jezreel in the wild ride before the deluge.

3. Study the passages in Proverbs that present Wisdom as a person (Prov. 3:13-18; 4:1-13; 8:1—9:12). Note that in this dramatic personification Wisdom is represented as a woman. What reasons occur to you for this? How do they challenge you to a wiser life and a deeper understanding of God? Remember that the Greek word for wisdom is feminine—"sophia"—and that it appears in the name of the historic church in Constantinople—Saint Sophia—"Holy Wisdom"—that still adorns the modern city of Istanbul.

4. Read consecutively several chapters of historical narrative in either the Old or New Testament. List the things mentioned—clothing, food, tools, weapons, gear of any sort, cultural objects. With the help of ABC, EBL, or other reference and source books available, judge what part women played in the growth, preparation, manufacture, sale, and use of these items. Visualize the intricate commerce and the detail of the market place that could offer all these for sale. If several persons are interested in the study, divide the chapters. Pool and discuss the information gathered.

Chapter Four

Across the Boundaries of Race

THE QUESTIONS regarding race relations are among the most insistent and vexing that confront modern society. The Christian Church has come to recognize that they test its fiber and resolution as few others do. Explosive factors of high potential lie near the surface in this area. Possibilities of great good—the development of mutual understanding and reciprocal enrichment of life in the groups involved—may come through a wise solution of the problems. A cold and harsh practicality may offer no satisfying answer to this palpitant human problem. Likewise, an uninstructed and shallow sentimentality may provide an equally disastrous attempt at solution. Only when the light of Christ's love gives us a forthright recognition of the basic verities and illumines the stark and sometimes horrid facts, may we discover the solution to fundamental human problems.

In the Bible one finds numerous instances of interracial contacts, varying widely between kindly integration and bitter antagonism. Curiously enough, a number of the most suggestive incidents involve women as definite factors of action on one side or the other. We shall consider some of these situations, confident that from them helpful conclusions may be drawn for our approach to the problem of race which we face directly today.

THE DAUGHTER OF PHARAOH

Mention has been made of Merris, princess of Egypt,

daughter of Rameses II, in connection with the saving of the life of the baby Moses.[1] She played a major role in that fascinating episode, and her tender and womanly feelings prompted brave action on her part.[2] She definitely violated the edict of her royal father ordering the death of every male baby born to a Hebrew mother.

Rameses had succumbed to that strange and fearful hatred of a weak minority which frequently has plagued dictators. His predecessors had enacted increasingly harsh regulations aimed at their Hebrew slaves. With almost unbearable rigor they had been forced to toil in heavy construction, both in cities and in irrigation projects in the Nile delta. Then Rameses promoted this most inhuman edict of all, which, if it had been scrupulously observed, would have extinguished the Hebrew people in a half-century.

We recall the strategem of Jochebed, the placing of the infant Moses in his floating cradle, Miriam keeping watch a short way off. When the baby was found the princess recognized him at once for what he was, remarking, "This is one of the Hebrews' children."[3] Yet, moved by her instinctive womanly pity for the helpless and doomed infant, she declared him to be hers, and made the careful plan with Miriam for his nursing until such time as she might receive him at the palace as her son. This breach of the royal edict, involving the crossing of lines of racial and social cleavage, is truly remarkable. There was no urge of religious fervor or idealism to prompt Merris to this heroic act. The elements of human compassion and instinctive womanly love were sufficient to override the obstacles.

Viewed in the beauty of its essential humanity, this

[1]See discussions in chapters I and II.
[2]Exod. 2:1-10.
[3]Exod. 2:6.

lovely heroism of Rameses' daughter demonstrates certain factors that must enter as integral parts of every successful interracial relationship. Mutual human respect was here, and not only the recognition of need, but also the glad and unselfish willingness to meet the need. There was no overweening generosity from above, and no inferiority complex from below. We note the daring to defy discriminatory regulations through the wise choice of substitute peaceful procedure. These principles appear in the pact of Merris, Miriam, and Jochebed. They are as powerful and vital in the vast areas of our modern problem, as in the simplicity of the beautiful drama enacted by the ancient Nile.

RAHAB OF JERICHO

Another deed of outstanding bravery, involving the clashing interests of religion, race, and war, emerges in Rahab's care of Joshua's spies at Jericho.[1] As a good general, Joshua had sent two clever young officers on a reconnaissance of Jericho—its terrain, approaches and defenses, and the temper and spirit of its inhabitants. They came to the city before Joshua moved his forces from Shittim, deep in Moab, east of the Jordan. The spies may well have been disguised as traders. In their search of the city, they came to the house of Rahab who gave them shelter. She descried them to be Hebrews, and was profoundly impressed that these men sought her for the furtherance of their hazardous mission.

The story of Jehovah's power and of his care for the Hebrews in the desert had traveled before them. The people of Jericho were on edge, and their king was apprehensive because of the rumors of Joshua's approach through Moab.

---

[1]Josh. 2; 6:15-25.

They were almost a defeated people before the Hebrews crossed the Jordan.

Rahab's judgment of the character of the spies and their method of dealing with her, apparently convinced her of the moral worth and of the overwhelming power of Jehovah. Quietly, on the roof of her house where it touched the city's wall, they lay hidden under the stalks of drying flax, while perhaps she alternately watched the sentries on the wall and whispered to her guests. Rahab there proclaimed her new faith in Jehovah, and Joshua's officers gave her their promise that she and her household would be spared when Jericho lay under assault. Then, by a stout scarlet rope that she had braided of her own flax, she let them down over the wall into the night. By a roundabout route through the wild mountain gorges that she had told them of, they made their way back for the report to Joshua. That same rope, bound into the window-frame, was to identify her house, and be the pledge of safety when the Hebrews broke through the gates to take the city.

The factors of religion, race, and social relations are intensely vivid in this instance. Something of a genuine sincerity, a natural feeling of truth and honesty, passed like a spark between the disguised Hebrews and this woman of notoriety. She knew them for what they were, and refused to betray them. They knew that she had pierced their disguise, and yet they trusted her word and were grateful for the risks she assumed for them. She, in turn, believed their pledge of safety for herself and her family in the midst of an approaching conflict. They were of antagonistic races who would soon open battle after which would emerge the terrible status of conqueror and conquered. Their languages and culture were diverse; she had been an idolater, while they were worshipers of Jehovah, to whom idols were an abomination—tremendous grounds for difference lay between them. But the straight-forward and human decency of the spies, and the intuition of Rahab were solid piers from which the bridge of mutual trust and co-operation could be flung to span the chasm.

Rahab's steadfast faith in Jehovah—the eager willingness to serve him, even daring to harbor the enemies of her people—has been singled out as one of the compelling instances of faith triumphant.[1] Not only does a later scriptural writer hail her bravery; another records her moral reclamation as involved in her act of faith. So complete was this moral rehabilitation that she became the honorable wife of Salmon (Salma),[2] who was probably one of the spies she had sheltered. Salmon appears to have settled somewhat south of Jerusalem, giving the name Bethlehem to the place.[3] Boaz was the son of Salmon and Rahab. He was noted in his generation as one of the strong men of Bethlehem.[4] From him, through his descendants Obed and Jesse, the genealogy of David is traced. And on a far later day there was to be born "in the city of David a Saviour, who is Christ the Lord"[5]—that same city that had been founded by Salmon, Joshua's young captain, when he took Rahab of Jericho there.

NAOMI, RUTH, AND BOAZ

Few periods in the course of biblical history were equal in fury, fire, pillage, hardship, and suffering, to that recorded in the books called Joshua, Judges, and I Samuel. Yet life persisted, as mankind has ever known it to do, even in the

[1]Heb. 11:31; Jas. 2:25.
[2]Ruth 4:20,21; I Chron. 2:11, 12; Matt. 1:4, 5; Luke 3:32.
[3]I Chron. 2:51.
[4]Ruth 2:4.
[5]Luke 2:11.

days of greatest devastation and darkest misery. Homes were founded, houses built, children came to be the joy of parents' hearts, seed was sown, the harvest was gathered and processed for use. Songs were sung, laughter was heard in the streets, men met to buy and sell property and goods. And the God of all was worshiped by his faithful people, he whose imperishable word had declared:

> While the earth remaineth, seedtime and harvest, and cold and heat, and summer and winter, and day and night shall not cease.[1]

After the capture of Jericho, Ai and other walled cities were attacked and taken by Joshua's forces. The land had been apportioned among the several tribes. They then attempted to possess it. Unequal success attended their efforts. Jerusalem remained in Canaanite hands until David, when king, took it. Other towns to the west were not easily captured, and the Philistines gradually established their bases in the line of strong cities they held along the southern coast. But southward from the hill country of Ephraim,[2] along the central plateau to the desert we now call Negeb, and eastward to the Jordan and the Dead Sea, Joshua's men effected the most nearly complete conquest that any part of Palestine then experienced. In this area Joshua lived his last few rather quiet years, and was buried. Deborah eventually followed him as judge, sitting beneath her palm tree at Beth-el.[3] It was in Beth-el that Samuel grew to be Israel's first true prophet.[3] It was the country of Saul, the first king, and of David whose city was Bethlehem. The growing Hebrew power and the brightest hopes for the future centered here as in no other section of the land.

For a generation or so after Joshua's passing, the territory

---

[1] Gen. 8:22.
[2] Ten to fifteen miles north of Jerusalem.
[3] The work of Deborah and the influence of Samuel were discussed in preceding chapters.

85

of Ephraim, Judah, and Benjamin enjoyed comparative peace, and remarkable tranquility. Deborah was active as judge and spiritual leader. Although the Canaanite king Jabin was gaining power in Esdraelon and the north, he had not yet ventured to threaten the southland. The eastern sons of Midian still confined their raids to the country close to the Sea of Galilee. The first units of Philistine invaders had captured from the Canaanites Gaza, Ekron, Ashdod on the coast, but they had hardly begun penetration of the narrow defiles leading up to the Judean plateau. In one of the unusually peaceful decades occurred the events which are related in simple beauty in the Book of Ruth.[1]

The lyric sweetness and idyllic charm of this short book have placed it among the choicest of all literature. The stark problems of famine, migration, foreign residence, toil, bereavement, loneliness, create a background against which Naomi, Ruth, and Boaz stand clearly limned as if expertly sculptured in high relief. Loyalty, love, sacrifice, rectitude —these traits attire the subjects as in the vestments of royalty. A certain timeless vitality glows in the strength of Boaz. Naomi's yearning is as old as the race and as modern as the present homeless migrants of Europe. The steadfast devotion of Ruth, evidenced in a winsome grace sufficient in the most delicate relationship, gives to her an immortal loveliness. The unnamed author of this tale has told a story of profound and searching meaning as well as of deathless beauty of character.

"Thy People . . . . My People"

Beautiful and lovely in many ways as is this vignette of Ruth, the most important element in our immediate study is that of its race relationships. The hardships of famine,

---

[1] This short and lovely prose-poem should be read without interruption.

probably caused by the failure of seasonal rains, resulted in migrations of families or tribes.[1] Failure of crops has been a prime factor in the movement of peoples since time began. In our day, astoundingly effective means of transportation have often mitigated the horrors of famine, but even yet its gaunt approach is dreaded in many parts of the world. So much the more was this true in the days of Elimelech and Naomi.

Under the pressure of famine, this couple with their sons already grown to young manhood, traveled eastward from Bethlehem, crossing the Jordan beyond the site of ruined Jericho, and toiled onward to the hardy uplands of Moab. This area has always been rich in grain fields,[2] and was evidently less affected then by the famine conditions than was Judah with its stony ground. Sorrow followed sorrow for Naomi in the successive deaths of Elimelech and of their sons, Mahlon and Chilion. These young men had married young women of Moab, Orpah and Ruth, and the widowed daughters-in-law abode with Naomi. Thus a decade of foreign residence was rounded out for Naomi of Bethlehem.

It had not been easy for these migrants from Judah to adjust themselves to the social customs, language, culture, and religion that obtained in Moab. The distance was not great in mileage. It was tremendous in the ethical and spiritual aspects of life. Apparently Elimelech and his family had become partially integrated: with the sons marrying Moabite maidens, a family unit was established. They were still, however, foreigners, and the imprint of the outlander was upon them.

---

[1] The entry of Jacob and his sons into Egypt, when Joseph was in power there, is a classic instance (Gen. 42 ff).
[2] While there on a visit, the writer was impressed by the fertility of the soil and the extent of cultivated areas in this region, now part of Trans-Jordan.

Among the chief factors of difference were religious faith and practice, and the peculiar pride of descent that was already evidencing itself among the Hebrews as a facet of their religious experience. The religion of Moab, as we understand it, was idolatrous, with strong tendencies toward the sensual at certain seasons of the year. The worship of Jehovah was utterly opposed to the licentious in religious observance, and idols were abhorrent. Naomi and her men kept true to their faith, even in Moab. Their example carried definite influence. We find Ruth rather proudly declaring, "Thy God shall be my God," as though such an act marked for her a very definite step upward and ahead in faith.

Even at best, Naomi, bereft of her husband and sons, was not at home in Moab. Orpah was dutiful, but was not prepared to leave her own people to journey into a new, strange loneliness at Bethlehem. On the other hand, Ruth loved Naomi profoundly, understood her well, and was eager to go with her, despite the unforeseeable events to be encountered in the strange land. Naomi had been the foreigner in Moab for a decade. Ruth was willing to venture being a foreigner in Bethlehem for all her remaining days. With vivid recollection of her own heartache and bitterness, Naomi sought to dissuade her. Ruth, however, had made the great decision, and she voiced it in words that all generations have treasured:

> Entreat me not to leave thee, and to return from following after thee; for whither thou goest, I will go; and where thou lodgest, I will lodge; thy people shall be my people, and thy God my God; where thou diest, will I die, and there will I be buried: Jehovah do so to me, and more also, if aught but death part thee and me.[1]

Ruth of Moab at Bethlehem

Upon her return to Bethlehem, Naomi found herself at

[1]Ruth 1:16, 17.

home, no longer the foreigner. Ruth, who had lived joyously with her own people of Moab, was now the stranger and outlander. Without doubt she had coached Naomi concerning various intimate Moabite customs. Now Naomi must instruct Ruth as to Hebrew usage and manners. This she did with great care. Wisely Ruth heeded every admonition. With alert eyes she observed how others conducted themselves. She gave herself to the hard toil of gleaning after the reapers—back-breaking, heavy work, with but chance and scant return. She carried herself with commendable dignity. Loyal to Naomi, scrupulous in conduct, industrious at work, earnest in the new religious customs, Ruth made a place for herself in the community, and the walls of separation between native and foreigner were effectively breached. With such wisdom and tact had Ruth conducted herself that the elders readily approved the formal legal act of Boaz in redeeming the estate of Mahlon and in taking Ruth in marriage to perpetuate the order of the family of Elimelech.

> And all the people that were in the gate, and the elders, said, We are witnesses. Jehovah make the woman that is come into thy house like Rachel and like Leah, which two did build the house of Israel . . . . .[1]

Rachel and Leah had come from tribes outside the Hebrew group. Rahab had been a Canaanite. Now, in her turn, Ruth of Moab was to enter the house of Israel, and of her was born Obed, grandfather of David the king.

In his commentary upon the Book of Ruth, Professor William C. Graham offers this conclusion:

> The social problem with which the author endeavored to deal is a live issue in our own day and will be to the end of time. One can hardly doubt that the universal acceptance of the principles laid down in this book in regard to the treatment of foreigners would result in increasing good will among men the world over.

---

[1] Ruth 4:11.

But perhaps the greatest lesson of the book is that the way to happiness lies through intelligent co-operation with others. The individual virtues possessed by each character would not have been sufficient in themselves to achieve the happy result. It is our human limitations, of which no one is free, which make us essential to each other. To give what we can give in gracious co-operation with those who can give what we cannot—this is the path by which we may best serve, not only our own age, but posterity.[1]

A HEBREW SLAVE GIRL[2]

During Elisha's prominence as a prophet in Samaria, Naaman was commander-in-chief of the armed forces of the king of Syria. He held his post of authority and influence by reason of his prowess and skill. Yet he was a leper. How leprosy had come to him, we do not know. By his indomitable courage he had thus far surmounted its agony to him and to his dear ones, and had overcome the terrific handicap it laid upon his public functions and his career.

In the course of one of the many border forrays that characterized the age, a company of his troops had returned with Hebrew captives. Among these was a young girl whose destiny it was to be passed to Naaman's household as a slave. She was trained to serve his wife, and appears to have become very acceptable in that duty. Without doubt she had suffered keenly in the brutal wrench from her home and in its despoilment. However, she had not let this rankle in her heart, and when she saw how bravely her master and mistress carried themselves in their own great distress, her young spirit was moved with sincere compassion. Thus she said to her mistress:

> Would that my lord were with the prophet that is in Samaria! then would he recover him of his leprosy.[3]

[1]ABC, article "Ruth," p. 380. Quoted by permission.
[2]II Kings 5:1-27.
[3]II Kings 5:3.

Naaman's wife eagerly grasped this suggestion. The royal permission was readily granted, and Naaman journeyed to Samaria to stand before the house of Elisha the prophet of Jehovah.

Elisha's instruction to Naaman was to go to the River Jordan and bathe seven times in its waters. Then would his flesh again be clean and wholesome, cured of the leprosy. This enraged Naaman, who had thought the prophet would publicly call on the name of Jehovah and then, with magic rites over his diseased body, complete the cure forthwith. Moreover, as he said in his racial pride:

> Are not Abanah and Pharpar, the rivers of Damascus, better than all the waters of Israel? may I not wash in them, and be clean? . . . . [1]

A wise and trusted servant remonstrated with the angry general:

> My father, if the prophet had bid thee do some great thing, wouldest thou not have done it? how much rather then, when he saith to thee, Wash, and be clean? [2]

Upon this, Naaman, controlling his anger and pride, went to the Jordan and fulfilled Elisha's formula—

> . . . . and his flesh came again like unto the flesh of a little child, and he was clean. [3]

Returning to Elisha, Naaman was deeply impressed by the prophet's steadfast refusal to accept any of the rich gifts proffered him. The Syrian professed supreme faith in Jehovah, and begged the privilege of taking back to Syria some earth of Palestine so that he might even there perform sacrifice to Jehovah. With this privilege granted, he returned to Syria and its court, cleansed in body, rejoicing in heart, with a new and deep sense of the reality of Jehovah in his soul. The prophet's last word was to echo long in his heart:

> . . . . Go in peace . . . . . [4]

---

[1] II Kings 5:12.
[2] II Kings 5:13.
[3] II Kings 5:14.
[4] II Kings 5:19.

Across the chasm between owner and slave, wealth and poverty, pride of public position and complete anonymity, Syrian general and Hebrew prophet, the miracle of humanity upheld by unwavering faith built the bridge of understanding and co-operation. Need ever comprehends need. Suffering provides its own sympathy for suffering. Devotion of slave and faith of prophet may overcome alien prejudice and vanity to provide a blessing that knows no boundaries of race or social status. Today, as then, the formula is in the keeping of those who serve and pray. And sometimes, as in this case, the person in whose hands the secret rests for action is an unknown disciple of the Living God. True to him may we ever be, as was this Hebrew girl rudely riven from her own home, but nonetheless eager in human sympathy and brave in faith and devotion to God.[1]

JESUS AND THE WOMAN
AT THE WELL[2]

. . . . and he must needs go through Samaria.[3]

Thus John indicates a certain urgency that required Jesus and his disciples to use the short but hated route from Judea to Galilee. In that day no Jew would travel through Samaria unless necessity compelled him. It is true that the road from Jerusalem northward to Galilee was direct and easy, with no great variations in altitude to overcome. But it took the traveler "through Samaria." Better by far was it to follow the arduous, much longer, brigand-infested and mountainous road down to Jericho, across the Jordan, then northward over the uplands east of the river and back

---

[1]Note the Saviour's reference to this incident in his utterance in the Nazareth synagogue (Luke 4:27).
[2]John 4:1-42.
[3]John 4:4.

92

again just below the Sea of Galilee. The difficulties of this route were apparent in the journey of Joseph and Mary to Bethlehem. Yet, these hardships and dangers were preferable to the offense to racial pride laid upon a person who had to take the way through Samaria.

All this animosity rooted far back in the past—when the northern tribes were taken captive and later, with the deportations from Jerusalem, the vacuum of the unoccupied land was filled by a forced settlement of alien groups from distant areas similarly conquered. These displaced people, settled in Palestine, asked for priests to instruct them in the faith and worship of Jehovah, the God of the land. Partial aid and training were grudgingly given. In the later restoration, they were denied access to the rebuilt Temple at Jerusalem. They accordingly built their own shrine near Shechem, [1] and worshiped Jehovah there. The Jews despised the formularies and ritual followed by the Samaritans, judging them to be alien, partial, and inaccurate. Across the long years the mutual resentment grew, until in Jesus' day it was manifested in a hatred and antagonism of intense degree.

John offers no clue as to the reason that compelled Jesus and the disciples to take the Samaritan road. Jesus himself would have felt no hesitancy in making the journey. But there must have been a reason of prime importance to win the assent of the twelve disciples to travel that way. Indeed, the necessity had arisen so suddenly that there had not been time enough to provide good Jewish food for the total distance. Reaching Sychar, the group found the necessity of going into the Samaritan town to secure such food as might be available, galling, for it was an accepted

[1]Ezra and Nehemiah give some information on this situation. Consult the Index in ABC for references to sections of various articles.

principle of action that "Jews have no dealings with Samaritans."[1]

The Amazing Conversation

With the disciples on their way to Sychar, Jesus remained quietly at the ancient well, a short distance from the town. This was the well established for public use by Jacob,[2] continuing through centuries sweet and wholesome, and with an adequate supply of water.[3] To the well, then, came a woman of the city to draw water. When Jesus asked her for a drink, she marveled that he would ask any favor of her:

> . . . . How is it that thou, being a Jew, askest drink of me, who am a Samaritan woman?. . . .[4]

She was no less astonished than a low-caste woman of India would be if a Brahmin were to ask her for food or drink.

Thereupon followed a conversation between Jesus and the woman, unique even in Scripture. She was of alert mind, eager and quick. Her replies were remarkable for their phrasing and emphasis. With direct statements she touched the two basic issues in the antagonism between their groups—racial descent and religious sanctions. Jesus met the challenges in such fashion as to disarm her completely while admitting her as a worthy individual into the joy and glory of the Father's universal love.

The woman's first thrust concerned the very touchy question of racial descent:

> Art thou greater than our father Jacob, who gave us the well, and drank thereof himself, and his sons, and his cattle?[5]

Ordinarily, a Jew, certainly a Jewish leader, would have bridled at such a remark. "Who is this Samaritan, to say

---

[1]John 4:9.
[2]Gen. 33:18-20.
[3]The site is revered to this day; and the water is cool and delicious.
[4]John 4:9.
[5]John 4:12.

'*our* father Jacob, who gave *us* the well'?[1] What effrontery! Do you not know, O Samaritan, that Jacob was father of the Jews, and not of the half-breed Samaritans, and that he gave the well to us, Jews, and not to you, interlopers?'' This was a favorite theme of argument, and it often led to blows.

Jesus ignored the racial argument. His reply made water the symbol of God's vast love springing up in human hearts.

> Every one that drinketh of this water shall thirst again: but whosoever drinketh of the water that I shall give him shall never thirst; but the water that I shall give him shall become in him a well of water springing up into everlasting life.[2]

With the conversation thus turned into the religious realm, the Samaritan woman had still another barbed arrow in her quiver. This was the Jewish claim of religious superiority:

> Sir, I perceive that thou art a prophet. Our fathers worshipped in this mountain; and ye say that in Jerusalem is the place where men ought to worship.[3]

The Saviour's reply is amazing:

> Woman, believe me, the hour cometh, when neither in this mountain, nor in Jerusalem, shall ye worship the Father . . . . . But the hour cometh, and now is, when the true worshippers shall worship the Father in spirit and in truth: for such doth the Father seek to be his worshippers. God is a Spirit: and they that worship him must worship in spirit and truth.[4]

Again the Master evaded the controversial issue. He showed, without hesitancy, the limitations and transitory character of all the physical aspects of worship, as he exalted the timeless vitality and world-wide inclusiveness of worship ''in spirit and truth.'' The tenderness of his use of the phrase ''the Father,'' as representing God, won the

---

[1]The italics are the author's.
[2]John 4:13, 14.
[3]John 4:19, 20.
[4]John 4:21-24.

woman's heart, even as the wideness of God's mercy included her in the infinite love of the Father.

With every thrust turned aside, and all the weapons of controversy demolished, she based her next remark on the common ground of hope that both Samaritan and Jew eagerly entertained:

> .... I know that Messiah cometh (he that is called Christ): when he is come, he will declare unto us all things.[1]

The Saviour's answer:

> .... I that speak unto thee am he.[2]

The thirst of her soul was satisfied with the Living Water. The hunger of her heart now knew the Bread of Life. Light and joy dispelled all darkness from her spirit. Instinctively her thoughts were for her friends. Leaving the water jar at the well curb, she ran back to Sychar to tell of the amazing Teacher who had wrought so great a miracle in her soul. The crowd followed her to the well, and after their own eager hearing of his words, "They besought him to abide with them two days." many believed on him there, as they said to the woman:

> Now we believe, not because of thy speaking: for we have heard for ourselves, and know that this indeed is the Saviour of the world.[3]

Despite her sex, and her debased social position, the Samaritan woman became an adequate witness of the Saviour. So completely was her own soul filled with "living water," that its vital stream flowed into the hearts of many others. This group of believers in Sychar, formed around the experience of the woman at the well, was, without doubt, focal in the early spread of the gospel in Samaria after Pentecost.

The principles here established by the Master, and his

---

[1]John 4:25.
[2]John 4:26.
[3]John 4:42.

incomparable method so perfectly illustrated in this episode, have ever been basic to the missionary enterprise of
the church. And this is true in the polyglot and interracial
areas of American cities and countryside, even as it is in the
far-flung continents of the world. The pride and hatred
of race expressed in discrimination against others shrivel
and disappear in the warm glow of the love of God expressed in earnest human words and service. The common
ground of every man's search for God provides sure footing
on the road along which all men may walk without fear
side by side.

SUGGESTIONS FOR FURTHER STUDY

1. Read the story of Jesus healing the Syrophoenician woman's daughter (Mark 7:24-30; Matt. 15:21-28). This incident is a beautiful revelation of the Saviour's innate courtesy towards women. Note that the Greek word "kunarion" literally means "little dogs" (of the household), puppies for the children, rather than the vicious half-wild pariah dogs of the streets. This is the same area where Elijah had experienced the generosity of the Sidonian widow in the days of famine.

2. Read the Book of Esther, considering that this is one of the earliest examples in literature of an historical novel written for racial propaganda purposes. With the sole exception of the king Ahasuerus, who was probably Xerxes, all the characters of the book appear to be fictional. Extensive records of his reign have come down to us, but we find no mention of any of the persons named in the book. Note the stratagem and trickery ruthlessly employed by both sides in the drama, and the fact that there is no religious appeal, or expression of broad humanitarian concern. God is not once mentioned in the entire book.

3. Study the parable of the Good Samaritan (Luke 10:25-37), making an outline of the attitudes of segregation on the one side, and of human kindliness on the other, as exemplified by the various characters. Consider the effect of Jesus, having indicated the despised Samaritan as the one motivated by human consideration and courtesy uncontaminated by racial prejudice.

4. Study and list further New Testament references to Samaria and Samaritans, such as are in Acts 1:1-9; 8:1-25. You may find others. Estimate their significance in the matter of race relations.

Chapter Five

Women and the Text
of the Bible

ONE OF THE MOST fascinating angles in the study of Scripture has to do with questions of authorship. Vivid light is thrown on the meaning of a book when the life and work of its author stand clearly determined. In the Old Testament, the books of the various named prophets (excepting Isaiah 40 ff and Daniel), and some of the Psalms that carry David's name stand in this category. The authorship indicated in the first three Gospels, in the Acts of the Apostles, and in nearly all of the letters ascribed to Paul, is practically unquestioned.

On the other hand, some of the most important books in the Old Testament are of composite character. Chief among these are the major historical books from Genesis through Chronicles. The keeping of official records, with the notation of the religious implications thereof, appears to have been a function of the prophetic and priestly groups. Various sequences are identifiable in the texts of the historical books, as the editors of these records, while checking with earlier sources and documents, introduced their own comments and interpretations. The Book of Psalms was probably compiled for use as the hymnal of the Temple. A wide range of authorship is quite evident in the superscriptions of the individual Psalms. The composite character of Proverbs is perfectly obvious.

A number of important books are anonymous—Job, Daniel, Isaiah 40 ff. Hebrews, being notable examples. The authorship of the Fourth Gospel is still debatable. Many competent scholars think it was the Apostle John. Others maintain that John the Elder, of Ephesus, was more probably the author. The validity and worth of this extraordinary record of the Saviour's life and teaching is in no way impugned by the fact that its authorship is indefinite. A similar situation prevails concerning Revelation, Hebrews, and a number of less important writings.

With the possible exception of Hebrews, no total book of the Bible appears to have been written by a woman. The social and intellectual position generally allotted to women in the biblical periods would have made literary leadership an almost unprecedented privilege. However, numerous noteworthy lyrics and songs of devotion, included in the appropriate sections of Scripture, are definitely the composition of women. Some of these persist in spiritual and inspirational value to our own day, and are worthy of our careful study.

MIRIAM'S SONG AT THE RED SEA

We have thought of Miriam as she conspired with Jochebed, her mother, for the preservation of the baby Moses' life. Her work as leader of the women, and as "prophetess" before all the people, has held our attention. We now recognize her as the first of all women of Scripture to have composed material so effective and valuable as to be recorded in the actual text of the Bible. She evidently possessed a marked poetic gift. Indeed, it may be that this faculty was one of the essential elements that led to her being called "prophetess," the first to bear that unusual title.[1] Much prophesy is cast in the form of poetry, and every significant Old Testament prophet possessed definite poetic talent.

---

[1]Six women are titled prophetess in the Bible.

100

With the decimation of Pharaoh's host in the Red Sea, Miriam and Moses led the people in the singing of her fervid chant of victory (Exodus 15). The song is included in verses 1 to 18, and the refrain is repeated in verse 21. The original form of the chant was probably terminated at verse 12, for the following section assumes at least a partial conquest of Palestine, verse 17 actually referring to the Temple, built by Solomon. The verses 13 to 18 were apparently added to Miriam's original in order to round it out for liturgical and congregational use at a later day.

Like much primitive verse of this type, her song began with a simple couplet to be repeated by the multitude as a refrain, after each stanza, rendered by a solo voice. The refrain would set the theme and purpose of the hymn—in this case, the praise of Jehovah for his victory over the enemy:

> Sing ye to Jehovah, for he hath triumphed gloriously;
> The horse and his rider hath he thrown into the sea.[1]

Miriam's stanzas would correspond to the verses indicated in our biblical text. There is no hint concerning the melody they sang. It may have been that of some ancient folk song that everybody knew, or, possibly, a new and stirring theme that had sung itself into Miriam's heart as she fashioned the song, stanza by stanza.

The scene is unforgettable. The stiff east wind had blown back the waters of the Red Sea all night until the land appeared:[2]

> And with the blast of thy nostrils the waters were piled up,
> The floods stood upright as a heap;
> The deeps were congealed in the heart of the sea.[3]

Across this land-bridge the Israelites had moved in the dark as rapidly as possible, yet without panic. The control

[1]Exod. 15:21.
[2]Exod. 14:21.
[3]Exod. 15:8.

established by Moses through the group of younger men he had designated as captains, and the inspired leadership of Miriam for the women and children had kept the host steady. From the distance charged the chariots and horses of Pharaoh. They had finally picked up the trail after Moses had baffled them by a change of direction in their flight.[1] At the streaking of dawn, when the rearguard of the Hebrews had completed the crossing, and the first elements of Pharaoh's chariots were on the land-bridge,

> . . . . the sea returned to its strength when the morning appeared; and the Egyptians fled against it; and Jehovah overthrew the Egyptians in the midst of the sea.[2]

Or, as Miriam sang about the reversal of the wind with the rising sun:

> Thou didst blow with thy wind, the sea covered them:
> They sank as lead in the mighty waters.[3]

Standing on the farther shore, in the glory of the rising sun, viewing the wreck of Pharaoh's chariots under the turgid waters, the children of Israel chanted Miriam's song. The solo voice, possibly Miriam's, intoned each stanza. The mighty voice of all the people sang the simple antiphony even after the concluding stanza:

> Thou stretchedst out thy right hand,
> The earth swallowed them.
>
> .   .   .   .
>
> Sing ye to Jehovah, for he hath triumphed gloriously;
> The horse and his rider hath he thrown into the sea.[4]

DEBORAH'S SONG OF VICTORY

The oldest collection of songs and records to which definite reference is made in Scripture is the "Book of the Wars of Jehovah."[5] This very early book provided valuable material

---

[1]See Exod. 12:37 and 14:1 ff.   [4]Exod. 15:12,21.
[2]Exod. 14:17.   [5]Num. 21:14.
[3]Exod. 15:10.

to the later Hebrew historians, for it carried back the chronicle of events, and the memory of the folk songs, quite close to the actual happenings. Evidently a large part of this writing was devoted to the preservation of the folk songs.[1]

Among primitive and early peoples poetry is in the form of the ballad. These lyrics are fashioned to preserve the memory of great events, those that seem to shape destiny. Frequently the capture of a fortified town, or the outcome of a fierce battle, constitutes the event so determinative of the future. This was characteristic of the Hebrews, as of other peoples. The deeds of the hero were hymned, and the returning warriors were acclaimed by music, song and the dance. We have considered Miriam's song, after Pharaoh's debacle at the Red Sea. We are now to read Deborah's Song of Victory,[2] which doubtless was one of the oldest poems preserved in the "Book of the Wars of Jehovah."

The student should pay close attention to the marginal readings as the English text of this song is read. In a number of places the original form of the Hebrew is obscure. It is no wonder that this is the case, when we consider the decades that elapsed between Deborah's composition of these choruses and their incorporation into the text of Judges as we have it. The broad sweep of the song is perfectly clear. Possibly a dozen short phrases are obscure, or almost untranslatable, as they stand. The fact that these difficult passages exist is indicative that the song, as we have it, experienced little editing by later scribes, and is very close to the original of Deborah's own singing. It is

---

[1] The remarks concerning the "Book of the Wars of Jehovah" are pertinent also for another early writing known as the "Book of Jasher" (Josh. 10:13, II Sam. 1:18, and possibly I Kings 8:12 f. The word "Jasher" probably means "heroes."

[2] Judg. 5:2-51.

one of the half-dozen oldest chapters in the entire Old Testament.

Praise of the active presence and victorious power of Jehovah constitutes the major theme. This was also true of Miriam's song, where Jehovah's control of the winds and the sea was primary. Here again, the triumph of Barak and Deborah issued from the entrance of Jehovah into the battle with Sisera. The skill of Barak as leader and the valor of his men are in the song. But it is Jehovah who achieved the victory. This is characteristic of early Hebrew songs. There is profound religious emotion in them, and an ascription of praise to Jehovah beyond that given to any leader or group engaged in the conflict.

> Hear, O ye kings; give ear, O ye princes;
> I, even I, will sing unto Jehovah;
> I will sing praise to Jehovah, the God of Israel.[1]

The tribes that entered not the battle are cursed because they came not

> To the help of Jehovah against the mighty.[2]

Reuben, Dan, Asher, sent no troops to the conflict. They are thus condemned:

> Curse ye Meroz, said the angel of Jehovah,
> Curse ye bitterly the inhabitants thereof,
> Because they came not to the help of Jehovah, ...[2]

It was essentially Jehovah's battle that was being fought. The valiant Hebrews were only his allies. Thus the victory was hailed as Jehovah's:

> So let all thine enemies perish, O Jehovah:
> But let them that love him be as the sun when he goeth forth in his might.[3]

The last section of the song—verses 24 to 30—constitute a hymn in praise of the treachery of Jael, the wife of Heber

---

[1]Judg. 5:3.
[2]Judg. 5:23.
[3]Judg. 5:31.

104

the Kenite. She it was who lulled the defeated Sisera into a sense of temporary security by granting him hospitality. Then Jael shattered the traditions of sanctuary, and slew him in his sleep. This is a cruel episode, quite bereft of any extenuation. That it found place in Deborah's paean but shows the primitive passions and the low scale of moral demand and conscience that prevailed. We shudder and recoil from this deliberate breach of the sacred laws of hospitality. Yet, with the dark record of our own epoch, there is not much we can say in criticism. Now, as then, only the grace and love of God lifts mankind from savagery.

Deborah called herself "a mother in [for] Israel."[1] This she truly was, shepherding her people through long years of quiet, but amazingly effective, leadership;[2] when the issue was joined, leading them forth under the direct command of Jehovah; confirming and strengthening their faith in Jehovah, by her own self-effacement in the flush of overwhelming victory. Through her there poured into the souls of her people "a fiery flood of faith."[3] After the completion of her task, the record declares, "The land had rest forty years."[4]

HANNAH'S SONG OF PRAISE

The protection of God's people in the miracle at the Red Sea was sung in Miriam's outburst of exultation. The heroism of Barak and his cohorts, brave allies of Jehovah, echoed in Deborah's battle song. In the quiet hymn ascribed to Hannah,[5] Samuel's mother, we enter the realm of personal devotion that underlay much of Hebrew religion even in the

---

[1]Judg. 5:7.
[2]Read the sections in our preceding chapters.
[3]*Personalities of the Old Testament*, p. 60.
[4]Judg. 5:31.
[5]I Sam. 2:1-1

harsh decades of the Judges. We have sensed its deep and peaceful quality in the sheer loveliness of the book of Ruth. We find it revealed again in this beautiful psalm, characteristic of Hannah's faith which we have honored in our study of her influence upon Samuel.

In the composition of the Bible the song of Hannah fared differently from those of Miriam and Deborah. The antiphonal chant of Miriam, with its stirring refrain sung at the Red Sea, was preserved practically as remembered, apparently with little change in structure. The short concluding section was added by later singers, when it was chosen for the liturgy of the Temple for use by the congregation. Given place in the ancient "Book of the Wars of Jehovah," Deborah's song of Jehovah's victory over Sisera was included in Judges with no apparent alteration of early idiom or word. It was not suitable for Temple use, and was accordingly kept in its original form direct from the thrilling historic event that called it forth.

Early peoples possessed little feeling for what we might call "the property rights of authorship." This modern concept we carefully protect by our laws of copyright. In biblical days what had been written or sung was common possession, and succeeding generations could alter or rewrite at will with perfect propriety. Hannah's devotional hymn evidently has been largely rewritten. Her psalm was so personal in its warmth and sincerity that for many it reached the depths of individual devotion. Its vivid utterance of a universal experience of devotion gave it a rather timeless appeal. For this reason, from time to time, psalmists and singers felt free to adapt it to their peculiar needs. It then became a notable song of faith such as multitudes in all ages have cherished. Living for centuries in the devotional life of the Hebrews, it was destined to find its supreme restatement in the exquisite song of Mary which we call the Magnificat.

Pre-eminent in Hannah's song is the sense of Jehovah's constant care of his people with the bestowal of immeasurably rich blessing upon those who steadfastly hold to him in faith:

> There is none holy as Jehovah;
> For there is none beside thee,
> Neither is there any rock like our God.
>
> . . . .
>
> He will keep the feet of his holy ones;
> But the wicked shall be put to silence in darkness;
> For by strength shall no man prevail.[1]

MARY AND THE MAGNIFICAT[2]

In the Beatitudes Jesus gave primary spiritual position to the "poor in spirit," to those who ever "hunger and thirst after righteousness," to the "meek" and "pure in heart." These phrases stress the incalculable worth of the singleness of purpose and dedication that link the devout believer with God, in which ever live the richest blessing, the ultimate felicity of the soul. From childhood, Mary of Nazareth, who was to become the mother of the Saviour, may have been of this group. Without doubt, she reached a maturity of soul rarely achieved, for when "the fulness of the time came, God sent forth his Son,"[3] born of her. Mary must have been familiar with the devotional literature of her people, as in words strongly reminiscent of Hannah's immortal psalm, she sang her most intimate meditation. She was to bring to birth the Saviour of the world. Hannah's son, devoutly prayed for, as a blameless priest, had purified the worship and devotion of the people, and in his function as prophet of Jehovah had established

[1] I Sam. 2:2, 9.
[2] Luke 1:46-55.
[3] Gal. 4:4.

107

the royal line of David in full dependence upon God. Mary's Son was to be Prophet, Priest, and King. Hannah's noble song must have had great meaning for Mary through the days of her earnest expectation, and across its strands of devotion she wove the tapestry of praise that bears her name:

My soul doth magnify the Lord,
And my spirit hath rejoiced in God my Saviour.
For he hath looked upon the low estate of his handmaid:
For behold, from henceforth all generations shall call me blessed.
For he that is mighty hath done to me great things;
And holy is his name.
And his mercy is unto generations and generations
On them that fear him.[1]

The Church is ever deeply indebted to the Gospel according to Luke for the record of this glorious song, and for the preservation of the other bursts of ecstatic praise closely associated with the birth of the Saviour—the Benedictus,[2] sung by Zaccharias, priestly father of John the Baptist; the utterance of the angel to the shepherds at Bethlehem, followed by the Gloria in Excelsis[3] of the full chorus of the heavenly host; the Nunc Dimittis,[4] chanted by the aged Simeon as he took the infant Jesus into his arms at the Temple. These four amazing songs are in the possession of the Church through the care of Luke, who deemed them worthy of permanent record.

In the introductory paragraph of his Gospel, Luke wrote to Theophilus:

.... it seemed good to me also, having traced the course of all things accurately from the first, to write unto thee .... that thou mightest know the certainty concerning the things wherein thou wast instructed.[5]

Luke was with Paul all of the two years of the apostle's imprisonment at Caesarea.[6] During that time he "traced

---

[1]Luke 1:46-50.
[2]Luke 1:67-79.
[3]Luke 2:10-14.
[4]Luke 2:25-35.
[5]Luke 1:3, 4.
[6]Acts 23 to 26.

the course of all things accurately from the first," as he had the opportunity of contact and fellowship with those who had been close to the Saviour. The writings of Luke would indicate that he was a man of gracious spirit, warm and friendly, truly Greek in his love of the beautiful in poetry, music, and art.[1] Luke may have known Mary, Jesus' mother, personally, for in writing the story of the Saviour's birth, he noted more than once how Mary "kept all these sayings, pondering them in her heart."[2] To Luke, Mary may have revealed these verities, so precious and wondrous, so intimately her own. With the natural delicacy granted to him, he could have won her confidence, learning from her these four glorious songs, and a multitude of thoughts and impressions that later he was to weave skillfully into his story of the Master's life.

A noted French scholar once called Luke's Gospel "The most beautiful book ever written."[3] There is rare beauty in it, and a blending of the human and divine in the Saviour that baffles analysis. It is Luke's marvelous tribute to the Master, but much of its singing quality and profound insight may reflect the influence of Mary's story and her own love of her Son phrased so exquisitely in her song of him before ever he was born.

HULDAH AND DEUTERONOMY

During the tumultuous and cruel reign of Manasseh (697-641 B.C.), the prophet Isaiah suffered martyrdom.

---

[1] There is a tradition found in very early church writings that Luke was an artist of no mean ability, and that his influence fostered an attitude of reverence previously unknown in art. At any rate, the incidents and teachings found only in the Third Gospel have influenced Christian art (painting and sculpture) to a remarkable degree. The author of material of such inspirational value to artists must have possessed a natural sense for an appreciation of art.

[2] Luke 2:19, 51.

[3] Renan: *"Le plus beau livre qu'il y ait."*

Politically, Judah was vassal to Assyria. Worship in the Temple had become very corrupt, with the startling introduction of the adoration of foreign deities and their idols. The true prophets of Jehovah underwent bitter persecution, culminating in the death of Isaiah. It was necessary for the devout leadership "to go underground," in our modern phraseology. Manasseh was followed by the scant three years of the worthless Amon. In 639, Josiah, his son, became king, to reign until 608, when he died locked in battle with the great host of Pharaoh Necho II, below the mighty fortress of Megiddo.

Josiah seems to have been predisposed to a purer worship of Jehovah and to a nobler way of life than his predecessors had been. He was but a lad on ascending the throne, and others at first ruled for him in a sort of regency. Coming to young manhood, he assumed the full power of kingship. This gave the apparently quiescent, but actually very vital followers of the older prophets the priceless opportunity for which they had ardently prayed and zealously striven. They achieved a coup d'etat among the most brilliant and far reaching in Hebrew annals.

A picture of the incredible moral depravity of the day is given in the sixth and seventh chapters of Micah. And, in the midst of his description of the sin that was so rampant, he uttered a call to spiritual consecration that constitutes as sublime a challenge as is found anywhere in the Old Testament:

> Wherewith shall I come before Jehovah, and bow myself before the high God? . . . . He hath showed thee, O man, what is good; and what doth Jehovah require of thee, but to do justly, and to love mercy, and to walk humbly with thy God?[1]

Micah prophesied for just a short time after the death of Isaiah, and then his voice, too, was silenced. But he appears

---

[1]Mic. 6:6, 8.

to have stimulated a movement, at first necessarily secret, then ready to seize the ascendancy at the right moment. Part of the work of the devout group he inspired was the editing of the ancient Law of Moses, and its interpretation for the tragic day in which they lived. Whether one outstanding person assumed the authorship, or a small committee worked in close collaboration, it is now impossible to say. The result of the effort, however, was the writing of the book we call Deuteronomy,[1] a work filled with profound spiritual insight, and destined to exert an influence vital and powerful for many centuries.

When finished, carefully reviewed and approved by the devout leaders-in-seclusion, the clandestine writing was deposited somewhere in the Temple to await the propitious moment for discovery. Meanwhile Josiah had been crowned as a lad, and had begun to evidence such faith and loyalty to Jehovah as heartened these hidden followers of the older prophets. One by one their friends came into important positions at the court. Shaphan become the royal scribe. Hilkiah was now high priest, evidently a just and righteous man. Harhas was keeper of the royal wardrobe, thus very close to the person of the young king. His grandson was husband of Huldah, noted as a prophetess before Jehovah. These, at least, we know. Others no doubt were in the royal entourage.

In his eighteenth year as king, Josiah ordered a strict accounting of the funds that had accumulated at the Temple, and he decreed they should be immediately used in the cleansing and restoration of the sacred building. This proved to be the moment for action. Hilkiah found the hidden scroll somewhere in the Temple, and sent it to the king by the hand of Shaphan his scribe.[2] Josiah ordered Shaphan to read it aloud before him.

---

[1]The word means "second statement of the Law."   [2]II Kings 22.

111

> And it came to pass, when the king had heard the words of the
> book of the law, that he rent his clothes. And the king commanded
> Hilkiah [and others] . . . . saying, Go ye, inquire of Jehovah for me,
> and for the people, and for all Judah, concerning the words of this
> book that is found . . . . .[1]

Apparently Huldah, as prophetess, represented the highest source of Jehovah's revelation, for the men went directly to her from the king's presence.[2] She gave prompt endorsement to the book as the valid word of God, and declared that its judgments were inevitable. She also voiced high commendation of Josiah for his tenderness of heart and loyalty to Jehovah, declaring that the ultimate woe and desolation would not come in his lifetime because of his humility.[3] Josiah proceeded at once to rid the Temple, and all of Jerusalem as well, of every defilement of the lustful idolatries that had besmirched the sacred place. He re-instituted the passover, and set an example for the people by his own acts of personal devotion and a righteous life.

Granted the fact of the book's supreme spiritual value given it by its devout authors; the devoted care that kept it safe in the Temple; the skill and determination whereby the priest and scribe gave it to Josiah; it was Huldah, the prophetess, who held its destiny in her hands. She gave assurance of its place in the most sacred element of Scripture —The Law. Her kind words to Josiah strengthened him in the re-establishment of Jehovah's worship, and the reformation of public life according to his statutes. Although she had no part to play in its writing, which may well have been completed before her birth, Huldah was responsible, as none other, for the authentication of this great book as part of the Word of God. Women of our day who find inspiration and strength in the deathless phrases

---

[1] II Kings 22.
[2] II Kings 22:11-13.
[3] II Kings 22:15-20.

of Deuteronomy may well be proud of the woman, in a place of leadership, who bravely placed it in the fore-front of her people's faith and practice.

For over two thousand years since Josiah's public proclamation every true Hebrew has bowed in reverence with the recitation of his creed:

> Hear, O Israel: Jehovah our God is one Jehovah. And thou shalt love Jehovah they God with all thine heart, and with all thy soul, and with all thy might.[1]

In his own day the Saviour was to declare this to be the first and great commandment, on which, with the second, "Thou shalt love thy neighbor as thyself,"[2] would hang all the law and the prophets.

For many generations the loyal people of Jehovah had sedulously trained their children in faith and devotion. We have thought of numerous mothers who had taught the divine truth to their little ones. This book was to provide the inalienable charter of all formal and personal religious education from that day even until ours:

> And these words, which I command thee this day, shall be upon thy heart; and thou shalt teach them diligently unto thy children, and shalt talk of them when thou sittest in thy house, and when thou walkest by the way, and when thou liest down, and when thou risest up.[3]

Deep into the souls of men has flowed the river of the strength of this book. The nearness of God, his boundless love and mercy, his immeasurable power, are the sure possession of those who love him with all their heart and soul and might. In the hour of his own fierce temptation, the Savior found overwhelming answer to Satan in these words:

> .... Man shall not live by bread alone, but by every word that proceedeth out of the mouth of God.[4]

---

[1]Deut. 6:4,5.
[2]Matt. 19:19 (Mark 12:31; Luke 10:27; Rom. 13:9), based on Lev. 19:18.
[3]Deut. 6:6,7.
[4]Matt. 4:4 (Deut. 8:3).

Thou shalt not make trial of the Lord thy God.[1]

Thou shalt worship the Lord thy God, and him only shalt thou serve.[2]

PRISCILLA AND THE EPISTLE TO THE HEBREWS

Writing about the year 225 A.D., Origen, noted scholar of the post-Apostolic Church, declared: "Who wrote this epistle to the Hebrews, God only knows." Indeed, several prominent early leaders in the Church, because of its evident anonymity, had hesitated to validate this epistle as Scripture of the same level of inspiration as the Gospels and the Pauline letters. Whatever may be the opinion of scholars as to the possible authorship of this book, there is general agreement on this point at least, that Paul could not have been its author.[3]

One of the most important versions of the Bible in English is known as the Geneva Translation. This was made in Geneva, Switzerland, in the late 1500's by a group of distinguished English scholars-in-exile. It passed through many printings and editions, being in wide popular use in England and Scotland prior to the preparation of the King James Version, which edition, in its actual composition, was largely based on the Geneva Translation. The following quotation, taken from the introductory statement to Hebrews in the Geneva Bible, is illuminating:

> Forasmuch as divers, both of the Greeke writers and Latines witnesse, that the writer of this Epistle for just causes would not have his name knowen, it were curiositie of our part to labour much therein. For seeing the Spirit of God is the author thereof, it diminisheth nothing the authority, although we know not with what

---

[1]Matt. 4:7 (Deut. 6:16).
[2]Matt. 4:10 (Deut. 10:20).
[3]The translators who produced the King James Version made an egregious error in ascribing Hebrews to Paul. This mistake was corrected in the American Standard Revision, which offers no ascription of authorship.

pen he wrote it. Whether it were Paul (as it is not like) or Luke, or Barnabas, or Clement, or some other, his chiefe purpose is to perswade unto the Hebrewes . . . . .[1]

Luther offered the brilliant thought that Apollos, who had come originally from Alexandria, might well be its author. Many recent scholars are inclined to look upon this as a wise suggestion, although the absence of definite evidence renders such a proposal not much more than a theory.

The epistle itself presents no clue in word, or description, or allusion. The personal characteristics of the author are, however, rather clearly indicated. He was probably of Hebrew lineage and training, for an intimacy with Hebrew religious custom and tradition is evidenced such as few Gentiles would have. The author was obviously a Hellenist, that is, of the Dispersion, born and reared outside of Palestine. A sympathetic and deep understanding of the philosophical ideas and terms current in the Greek world is displayed. The writer possessed marked literary ability, writing in Greek with a facility and power unmatched in the entire New Testament, save by Luke. Not only is the epistle a classic in style, it reads aloud superbly, showing that the author was a skilled public speaker, or preacher. The writer must have had a passionate devotion to the Saviour, a complete loyalty to him as the Son of God, and a tremendous concept of the supremacy of the cross. The description of Apollos gives strong ground for Luther's proposal.[2]

A much more recent theory advances the authorship of Priscilla. This has been advocated by scholars as eminent

---

[1]This quotation is from a Bible that belonged to Philip Embury, who established the first Methodist Society in America, in New York City, in 1766. This Bible, printed in 1611, is a copy of the Geneva Translation (printed in 1560), of the rare edition known as the "Breeches Bible." It is preserved at the John Street Methodist Church in New York, the present-day successor of Philip Embury's original society.

[2]Acts 18:24-28 (also reference in I Corinthians).

as Harnack, Rendel Harris, and Peake. Priscilla may be the answer to the question of authorship. Indeed the very fact that no name was ever attached to the epistle, even in the earliest days, has been used as an argument in favor of Priscilla. That she was a woman might have been considered as militating against the acceptability of the letter to those to whom it was actually addressed.

In this question of authorship nothing more definite can be said for Priscilla than can be adduced in favor of Apollos. The names stand as about equal in choice, and each one is favorably considered by many competent scholars of our day. Except for the scant possibility of Barnabas, no other name is given any strong consideration in this question of authorship.

It is recorded that "when Priscilla and Aquila heard him [Apollos], they took him unto them, and expounded unto him the way of God more accurately."[1] The ministry of Apollos, so fruitful in the Church, flowered from his own rich personality. Devoted in deepest loyalty to Christ, he received his training in the wise counsel and deliberate schooling of Priscilla and Aquila. When some of the best scholars suggest that in greatest likelihood either Apollos or Priscilla wrote this proclamation of the faith, they are really saying that Priscilla was influential to a very high degree in this period of Christian writing. This letter is an early attempt to state the spiritual facts of Christianity in terms of organized philosophy.

The theme is in the first sentence:

> God, having of old time spoken unto the fathers in the prophets by divers portions and in divers manners, hath at the end of these days spoken unto us in his Son . . . . .[2]

The perfect salvation of God is proclaimed:

---

[1]Acts 18:26.
[2]Heb. 1:1,2.

Wherefore also he [Christ] is able to save to the uttermost them that draw near unto God through him, seeing he ever liveth to make intercession for them.[1]

How much more shall the blood of Christ, who through the eternal Spirit offered himself without blemish unto God, cleanse your conscience from dead works to serve the living God?[2]

Christ is the potent root of our faith:

Now faith is assurance of things hoped for, a conviction of things not seen.[3]

. . . . let us run with patience the race that is set before us, looking unto Jesus the author and perfecter of our faith . . . . .[4]

Now the God of peace, who brought again from the dead the great shepherd of the sheep with the blood of an eternal covenant, even our Lord Jesus, make you perfect in every good thing to do his will, working in us that which is well-pleasing in his sight, through Jesus Christ; to whom be the glory for ever and ever. Amen.[5]

WOMEN LEADERS OF TODAY

Comparatively few of us are endowed with the genius of creative ability. We cannot all write or sing, paint or play, compose music or sway multitudes by the power of speech. In the spiritual implications of this fact, Paul is careful to note the worth of the various gifts of the Spirit:

And having gifts differing according to the grace that was given to us . . . . .[6]

. . . . Howbeit each man hath his own gift from God, one after this manner, and another after that.[7]

Now there are diversities of gifts, but the same Spirit. And there are diversities of ministrations, and the same Lord. And there are diversities of workings, but the same God, who worketh all things in all. But to each one is given the manifestation of the Spirit to profit withal . . . . . but all these worketh the one and the same Spirit, dividing to each one severally even as he will.[8]

---

[1]Heb. 7:25.
[2]Heb. 9:14.
[3]Heb. 11:1.
[4]Heb. 12:1,2.
[5]Heb. 13:20,21.
[6]Rom. 12:6.
[7]I Cor. 7:7.
[8]I Cor. 12:4-7, 11.

117

> And he gave some to be apostles; and some, prophets; . . . . till we all attain unto the unity of the faith, and of the knowledge of the Son of God, unto a fullgrown man, unto the measure of the stature of the fulness of Christ: . . . .[1]

> Now ye are the body of Christ, and severally members thereof.[2]

In the body, to which Paul thus likened the Church, the eye is intensely important, but it is small in size. The sense of hearing, highly and marvelously specialized, operates in a small area. The vocal chords, without which speech and song would be impossible, are not large in comparison with other factors in the throat. In a closely restricted section of the brain the chief co-ordinating centers of perception, judgment, and action appear to be located. The tiny coil-like canals of the inner ear determine our sense of equilibrium. Who has touched the delicate mechanism of the body's thermostat? How great is the mass of the body in comparison with the units where consciousness resides, creative ability functions, impulses are generated, and volitional control exercised!

Thus it is also in the Church. Here are those who see, think, judge, inspire, control, lead. These are few, even though they be the shapers of destiny. We, the many, who are bone and muscle of the Church, follow them. It is theirs to judge and lead. It is ours to follow in their train, strong to carry the burden, brave to endure, determined to achieve the goal that they, our eyes and ears and heart and thought, have planned in the Spirit of God.

Just as the orator or musician must have his audience, and the artist and the poet his public, so the creative leader in the Church must have his earnest followers and helpers. The audience, *en rapport* with the violinist, helps to create the masterpiece. The understanding public inspires the artist in the very process of secret creative effort. So does

[1]Eph. 4:11, 13.
[2]I Cor. 12:27.

118

the receptive and eager church surround its leader with an atmosphere of devout anticipation that enters deeply into his soul in the exalted moments of spiritual perception.

Miriam stood exultant for Jehovah at the Red Sea, but it was the controlled courage and the deep-voiced unanimity of the people that made her song supreme. Deborah knew the tribal men at her side, and in the midst of fierce battle she heard the melody she had taught them in the full-throated bugle, and in the salute of a man who had stopped a chariot of Sisera single-handed. The quiet, simple melody of Hannah evoked such chords of response that it filled the Temple with praise for centuries before Mary immortalized it in her glorious aria of consecration that will be sung wherever the Church abides.

The multitude, humbled and contrite, joined in the Passover when resumed by King Josiah, fulfilling the eager hope of the men who had written in desert caves, and of the prophetess, Huldah, who was unafraid in her declaration of Jehovah's righteousness, and very tender in her blessing of the king. Priscilla may have inspired and Apollos may have written the amazing Epistle to the Hebrews; yet it was the Church that answered to the challenge by its dedication to faith triumphant.

The Church today is proud of the women who stand in posts of creative leadership. And they, in turn, are buoyed up and greatly strengthened by the many who follow in the trails they blaze.

SUGGESTIONS FOR FURTHER STUDY

1. Write Hannah's song and Mary's Magnificat side by side, line for line. Compare them carefully. Note how the one may have inspired the other; and, yet, how each is complete and individual in its own right.

2. Study the material in Luke's Gospel that he alone gives. The passages can be readily found in a good synopsis of the Gospels, or by a study of the marginal references in your Bible. Note particularly the teachings of the Saviour, or special incidents that you think Luke may have learned from Mary. Evaluate her possible contribution to the writing of this Gospel.

3. The following women are named "prophetess" in Scripture: Miriam (Exod. 15:20); Deborah (Judg. 4:4); Huldah (II Kings 22:14, II Chron. 34:22); Noadiah (Neh. 6:14, and compare Ezek. 13:17); the wife of Isaiah (Isa 8:3); Anna (Luke 2:36). Study their lives to find what characteristics they held in common, and what would separate the one who was of evil intent (Noahdiah) from the others.

4. Look up in *The Methodist Hymnal* the hymns written by women, using the index of authors and the index of composers in the last pages of the hymnal. At least ten women are listed among the composers, and a much larger number as authors. Construct and use a worship service planned around the music and lyrics of women in the hymnal, and the writings of women in the Bible.

5. Make your own honor roll of women of the Church who you think have rendered service worthy of this distinction.

Chapter Six

Women of Prayer, Faith, and Service

THE ESSENCE OF PRAYER

Prayer is the Christian's vital breath,
The Christian's native air . . . . .[1]

Thus James Montgomery sang of prayer, and his hymn is one of the most notable in the poetry of devotion. Prayer is as instinctive, and should be as natural, as the act of breathing. It underlies all types of religion and religious experience. The forms and patterns that prayer may take are as multitudinous as the varieties of religion men have followed. But the essential nature of prayer abides ever with men and women across the uncounted years and the vast earth.

As there are two functions in the act of breathing, there are likewise two in prayer. Expiration in prayer is man reaching out to God. Montgomery again phrases it for us:

Prayer is the simplest form of speech
That infant lips can try;
Prayer the sublimest strains that reach
The Majesty on high.[1]

Prayer, as commonly understood, is the expression of the soul's deepest desire, the song of exaltation and ecstatic praise; the cry of the sinner; the meditation of the saint; the intercession of the burdened soul for one in great dis-

---

[1]See *The Methodist Hymnal*, No. 303.

tress. These all are the speech of the soul to the Father.[1]

Yet, in breathing, inspiration alternates with expiration. The parallel is absolute for prayer. There must be inspiration, the reception of spiritual concepts, before we dare to speak with God, the filling of the soul with the sense of his pure presence ere we may venture to "make all . . . . [our] wants and wishes known." The reading of the Book, quiet meditation, spiritual silence, the receptive attitude, knowledge that we are but empty vessels till he fills our spirits—these promote the inspiration of the soul. They are as fundamental a part of prayer as is utterance or petition. Indeed, the soul must know God and his abiding presence, before there can be adequate power for praise or asking. Let the inspirational aspect of prayer purify the heart and strengthen the soul, and the abundant grace and satisfying power of private or public prayer will follow as the day the night.

EARLY BIBLICAL DEVOTION

We have noted how personal devotion entered deeply into the life of the Hebrew people, even in the earliest days. Abraham and Sarah, Jochebed and her family, Hannah and Samuel, were persons to whom prayer meant very much. As the community grew, during the leadership of Moses and Joshua and Deborah and Samuel, we observed the steady development of prayer and devotion throughout the group. This came to flower under the inspired minstrelsy of David, reaching full fruitage in the elaborate ritual of the services in the Temple, instituted by Solomon. The glory of individual prayer and faith was not lost. Rather, it

[1]Read the sections, "In the Beginning" and "Fulfilment," in Dr. Charles Laymon's *Great Prayers of the Bible*, published by the Woman's Division of Christian Service.

became a powerful companion to the liturgy of an elaborate priestcraft, the sacrificial system that tended to blend many rich personal strains of devotion into a great, almost impersonal, act for all the people as a unit.

At first thought the field within which women could exercise their natural instinct for prayer might appear to be very restricted. In the long years, however, it proved to be fertile ground. From their steadfast faith and personal experience of God, there developed an attitude toward religion and its forms of worship quite unparalleled in their day. Although there was the ever-present temptation to follow idolatrous forms and adopt impure practices, a "remnant" always held true to Jehovah and the historic forms of worship in his name. Members of this group strove to maintain such purity of life and habit as he required.

The men who were destined to become the noblest leaders of Hebrew thought and religious custom had enjoyed youthful training in the constant faith and devotion of their homes. This household phase of worship, conducted, it is true, by the men, was constantly supported and reinforced by the loyalty of the women. Because of what they represented in Hebrew society, on a high social plane, in comparison with their pagan sisters, the devout Hebrew women came to assume a quiet but necessary and effective function in the worship services of the home and community, that of lending inspiration to the head of the house.

As the centuries passed, the Messianic hope of the Hebrew people became fixed as a sort of magnetic pole around which much of their devotional life was organized. Men eagerly looked for the Messiah, and prayed for his coming, with the yearning hope, each time a son was born, that *he* might prove to be the Anointed. This devotion kept them steady through the terrible decades of persecution and suffering from the time of Alexander the Great to the Roman occupation, to the very day of the Saviour.

WOMEN IN THE EARLY CHURCH

In the first half-century of the Christian Church, recorded in measurable detail in the last chapters of the Gospels, in Acts and in the letters of Paul, of John and in the Epistle to the Hebrews, women were privileged to assume leadership in spiritual things to an extent that their earlier sisters had hardly known. These Christian women were, at first, mentioned as belonging simply to the congregation:

> These all with one accord continued steadfastly in prayer, with the women, and Mary the mother of Jesus, and with his brethren.[1]

Later, at the Day of Pentecost, and on other great spiritual occasions, the use of the inclusive word "all" appeared to signify the effective presence of numbers of women in the congregation receiving the amazing gifts of spiritual power equally with the men. Paul, on a day, was to declare that there were no differences of race, nationality, social status, or sex, that should separate the Church into varying strata of privilege or obligation.[2] All were to share without such consideration in grace, opportunity, and responsibility.

One early concern of the Church was for the proper care of the aged, the infirm, and for those widows who could not easily provide for themselves. The solicitude for such prompted the designation of devout men like Stephen, Philip, Prochorus, and others to superintend this labor of love.[3] Much of the service entailed was doubtless carried forward by consecrated women. The spiritual power of women, devout in faith and prayer, pent up for so long in

[1]Acts 1:14.
[2]Gal. 3:26-28.
[3]Acts 6:1-7.

the eager hearts of the women of the Hebrews, found these new channels of expression in the early Church. The beautiful flowering of this spiritual grace had its roots in the assiduous care and receptive power of the Hebrew home developed from primitive days with sincere devotion and earnest prayer.

WOMEN AT PRAYER IN THE CHURCH TODAY

In the modern Church many doors leading to effective prayer-experience stand open to woman. The home, with its priceless opportunities of spiritual guidance, is her heritage. Through the development of the church school and kindred types of religious education, many women exercise this holy privilege with children and young people of families other than their own. The integration of women in the life and service of the Church provides opportunity for all of them to lead groups in acts of devotion. Numbers of women, feeling the direct call to such service, have been received into the ranks of the clergy and its affiliated offices—deaconesses, directors of religious education, pastors of rural charges, writers and editors of spiritual and devotional material, executives of organized religious work, missionaries at home and abroad. In each of these spheres of effort women now stand forth as leaders in worship and devotional exercise, true priests and prophets before the people.

These types of service all involve leadership in public prayer. For this there must always be earnest searching of heart and the constant guidance of the divine Spirit. The disciple, privileged to lead others in worship, stands ever in holy reverence before the Lord, quietly awaiting the word of inspiration, humbly praying to be Spirit-filled.

The supreme function of the older Hebrew women, gloriously fulfilled in the Early Church, is still the inheritance of present-day women. Peculiarly is it theirs to receive the quiet flow of spiritual experience. From this constant reservoir the expressive power of the Church's prayer may then be released.

> O Thou, by whom we come to God,
>   The Life, the Truth, the Way;
> The path of prayer Thyself hast trod:
>   Lord, teach us how to pray![1]

PRAYER AND FAITH

Prayer and faith move ever side by side on life's road of vivid experience. Each strengthens the other. There must be faith, at least of a sort, before any genuine prayer can be expressed or the reception of a blessed answer experienced. In the immortal Charter of Faith, the writer of Hebrews phrases it:

> . . . . without faith it is impossible to be well-pleasing unto him; for he that cometh to God must believe that he is, and that he is a rewarder of them that seek after him.[2]

With the growing sense of God's nearness that continuing prayer ever gives, faith is strengthened in the new conviction of God's reality, and is broadened in scope and deepened in understanding. As faith grows from experience to experience, prayer becomes more positive in accent, more receptive. Thus faith and prayer stride out together into the testing aspects of life. Suffering and sudden sorrow, gladness in life's joys, unheralded temptation, the trudging load, the challenge of high duty, bitter loneliness, the warmth of love's devotion—these all call forth meaningful prayer and faith. As faith and prayer chart the road before us, these widening ranges of life are brought into the in-

[1]James Montgomery, *The Methodist Hymnal*, No. 303.
[2]Heb. 11:6.

fluence of religious experience and power. Religious knowledge and certainty are built for us upon the foundation laid by prayer and faith deep in the soul.

Faith is the outgo of the total personality in such trust in God as gives to him all we are and have, and rests with him all we ever hope to be. Writing to Timothy from his final imprisonment, summing up the rich experiences of his apostleship, Paul declared:

> For which cause [the testimony of our Lord] I suffer also these things: yet I am not ashamed; for I know him whom I have believed, and I am persuaded that he is able to guard that which I have committed unto him against that day.[1]

It was Samuel's first glow of faith of this sort which he manifested when, as a lad, sleeping before the ark in the temple of Shiloh, he replied to the unfamiliar voice of Jehovah:

> . . . . Speak, for thy servant heareth.[2]

This was his own youthful dedication, confirming that which in faith his mother, Hannah, had made for him even before his birth. Across long years faith grew in him so that when the later historians of his people wrote of his service, they said:

> And Jehovah appeared again in Shiloh; for Jehovah revealed himself to Samuel in Shiloh by the word of Jehovah. And the word of Samuel came to all Israel.[3]

We watched the faith of Ruth of Moab develop until she left all she had known to throw in her lot with Naomi and the people of Jehovah, declaring:

> . . . . thy people shall be my people, and thy God my God.[4]

In contrast with the peaceful decade in which Ruth made her supreme choice, we beheld the faith of Rahab of Jericho

---

[1]II Tim. 1:12 (1:8).
[2]I Sam. 3:10.
[3]I Sam. 3:21—4:1.
[4]Ruth 1:16.

stand firm in the heat of battle and the appalling catastrophe of her city.

FAITH AND LOVE

The crown is given to faith when love becomes its motive and its strength. The intellectual element, just in itself, may be rather cold and impersonal. The sense of moral demand may give to faith a power to fulfill duty and obligation. It is love that illumines faith with personal meaning, that kindles in it the glow of adoration and wonder, that energizes it with the power that "never faileth."[1] Faith has gone a long distance on its journey when a person begins to think God's thoughts after him,[2] as if they were his own, when his great desire is to know the truth, so that the truth may set him free. A tremendous area of life is possessed when conscience joins with faith, and, cleansed by his grace,[3] takes control of righteousness. The will, guided by the truth of God and prompted by the now alert conscience, is empowered by faith to achieve the good.[4]

The supreme experience of faith is when love grants the sense of oneness with God, achieves the glory of adoring devotion, and floods the soul with light and power. This is the perfection of religious experience,[5] the goal of all our seeking. With the writer of Deuteronomy we love God with all the heart, and with all the soul, and with all our strength.[6] We now have

> . . . . access by faith into this grace wherein we stand; and we rejoice in hope of the glory of God . . . . because the love of God hath been shed abroad in our hearts through the Holy Spirit which was given to us.[7]

---

[1] I Cor. 13:8.
[2] II Cor. 10:5.
[3] Heb. 9:14.

[4] John 4:34; 7:17 (Cf. Rom. 7:18—8:4).
[5] I John 2:5; 4:17, 18.
[6] Deut. 6:5.
[7] Rom. 5:2, 5.

LOVE AND SERVICE

Love always must find ways of expressing itself in selfless service. Whatever may be the beauty of love's utterance in words, its true eloquence appears in the royal deeds of devotion. We treasure the memory of exalted hours in our homes, and the priceless possession of sacred gifts from the untold wealth of love's storehouse. These golden deeds were so purified in the fire of devotion that not a trace of the base alloy of selfish interest was in them. This being fact within the realm of human contacts, how blessed the love that fills the soul and God! How boundless the measure of his love!

> For God so loved the world, that he gave his only begotten Son, that whosoever believeth on him should not perish, but have eternal life.[1]

This love of God for all men, and for all mankind, we find personalized in such a way, and it becomes individual to each of us so perfectly in the Saviour, and in his Cross, that we can adequately answer only with the total devotion of which we individually stand capable. The command of Deuteronomy has become the glad response of our deepest nature when "we love him because he first loved us." Fear is banished, and love comes to its perfection over all of life.[2]

Our love for God is expressed in our worship of him. This may be in hymns of praise and in audible prayer of a congregation. It may be in the quiet meditation and devout prayer of an individual or of a close-knit family group. We have watched with reverence as the women of the Hebrew tribes and of the Early Church expressed their love of God in the forms of worship natural to them. Their faith has

[1]John 3:16.
[2]I John 4:7-21.

129

challenged ours, and the sincerity of their prayers and hymns has been an inspiration to us.

Love for God must also serve him. The spiritual aspect of worship calls for equal expression in the practical ways of daily living. The soul's devotion, the pure affection of the heart, the nobility of the mind attuned to the thoughts of God, marvelous though they be, are yet not enough. Loving-kindness that lifts those in distress, that defeats evil among men, the brave and selfless deeds that build God's kingdom in the earth—these are the proof of the soul's adoring love for God.

THE TASK FOR GOD'S PEOPLE

The better part of two thousand years had elapsed between the patriarchal days of Sarah and Abraham, and the vivid cosmopolitan era of Priscilla and Aquila, and of Lydia at Philippi. The political organization of the Mediterranean world had completely changed. Conquerors had come from the north and the west, and the ancient landmarks and boundaries were only a memory. The conquerors had brought strange languages, cultural ideas, and religions. Barter's simplicity was fast disappearing as the new complexities of commerce, industry, and world-finance emerged. No longer was the center of civilization somewhere along the Euphrates, the Tigris, or the Nile. Rome on the Tiber now governed the world.

These vast and fundamental changes in the world's life are reflected on the pages of Scripture. Many of the decisive events occurred within the experience of the Hebrew people, or had created the social and political ferment into which the Early Church was to venture. Vivid descriptions of many of the very happenings are in the Bible. Shrewd and profound analyses of the wide-ranging trends are in the words of prophets and apostles. This is an eternal function of the people of God—to live heroically, loyal to him, in the midst of civilization's growth or fall; to test fearlessly each old social habit, and each new procedure, by the ageless truth of God; to be that vital center of creative life around which shall be organized the kingdom of God in all the earth. The Saviour made searching declaration of this:

> I pray not that thou shouldest take them from the world, but that thou shouldest keep them from the evil one. They are not of the world, even as I am not of the world. Sanctify them in the truth: thy word is truth. As thou didst send me into the world, even so sent I them into the world.[1]

> . . . . The kingdom of heaven is like unto leaven, which a woman took, and hid in three measures of meal, till it was all leavened.[2]

And the seer whose vision penetrated to "that far-off divine event towards which the whole creation moves," hailed it in the ecstatic cry of the "great voices in heaven":

> . . . . The kingdom of the world is become the kingdom of our Lord, and of his Christ: and he shall reign for ever and ever.[3]

In their efforts to lift the world's life to higher levels, the people of God have found themselves intimately immersed in the common affairs of men. It is not so much by caustic criticism from without that they have made their achievement, although the direct challenge to base elements in life must not be evaded; it is rather by a sympathetic understanding of the problems of men and a sincere desire to share in the solution of them that ground is gained.

The consciousness of God's nearness is always necessary. The fact that the task we assume is his, and that the triumph of his kingdom is our goal, lends strength and courage. Prayer, ensuring his vital presence and might; faith, daring

[1]John 17:15-18.
[2]Matt. 13:33.
[3]Rev. 11:15.

131

to claim for him areas of life yet unattained; love, over-coming hardship, suffering, and every mortal adversary—these are the spiritual powers whereby we strive. Whether faithfulness in the simple humdrum of nomad society that was Sarah's, or the hardihood of Deborah; the reformation of a debased society that was Huldah's duty; or the nurturing of the infant Church that was the privilege of Mary of Jerusalem—the task, at root, was ever the same. Today, this task is ours also. And it requires of us, as of them, prayer which links our life with God, faith which sees the invisible and dares the impossible, love which is life's mightiest power, service which builds his reign of love in the world.

WOMEN OF SCRIPTURE AND SERVICE

No two women of those whose names we have called faced identical situations. Each lived her own life, with such faith and consecration as she was able to give. Some knew wealth, some continuous poverty. To a few was given the place of leadership of a multitude, with the fierce light of public life playing upon them. Others never moved far beyond the ranks of that uncounted multitude, appearing as symbols of the numerous anonymous members of society. The quiet simplicity of a little town was home for certain of them. There were those who moved ever along the great roads, by land or sea, and spoke the varying dialects of men in thronging cities. One might have been a queen. Another was a slave girl torn from her home in a border foray. Mothers have shown us the beauty of the home's devotion, and their joy in the precious lives given to them by God. Some, as strangers from afar, have faithfully represented the business interest of their distant homelands. The names of some are synonyms of faith and service, of faithfulness and tender compassion. The immortal songs of others are still our inspiration.

Through all the kaleidoscopic change of circumstance and responsibility that has passed before us, the service of God, sustained by faith and prayer, motivated and glorified by love, has controlled each pattern of action. In whatever specialized sphere these women of God found themselves, they knew his presence, they gave him their loyalty with ardor and devotion. Adjusting themselves to the shifting social order from generation to generation, these women knew that the highest plane of living was on the level of God's kingdom. They kept alive the sense of God's vital presence and strove to relate life's demands to his. The advancing knowledge of the world led them on to deeper, more satisfying thoughts of God, to the wider implications of his will and love for all mankind.

The achievement of an individual has held our admiration here or there. The personal devotion of another has helped us solve our own vexing problem. Basic to each, fundamental to all, is the sense of the nearness of God, the joy of prayer and communion with him, faith in him supreme, service for him the crown of life's accomplishment. They lived nobly, for in him they lived and moved and had their being.

THE WOMEN WHO MINISTERED TO THE SAVIOUR

At the outset of his description of Jesus' Galilean ministry, Luke indicates that a number of women were included in the group of the disciples.[1] The direct statement is made that these ministered to the Saviour "of their substance." Salome, the mother of John and James, may well have been

---

[1]Luke 8:1-3.

among them. Although Luke does not here mention her by name, she is included in this company on other occasions.[1] Mary, the wife of Clopas, may also have been one of them. She was sister to Mary, the mother of Jesus, and stood with her close to the Cross on Calvary.

Specifically, Luke here mentions three women, Joanna, the wife of Chuza who was Herod's steward, Susanna, and Mary of Magdala. Susanna is not personally identified at any other point in the Gospels. Luke names Joanna as one of the women who went with Mary of Magdala to the tomb early on Easter morning.[2] Being the wife of Herod's steward, she was evidently a person of influence, with some means at her disposal. These all were Galileans, and of that group who had close friendship with the Saviour as he came and went through the towns bordering the Lake.

It is instructive to note that all these were bound to Jesus by ties of loyal affection because of what he had done for them personally. Luke describes them as "certain women who had been healed of evil spirits and infirmities."[3] The power of prayer and the assurance of faith had been granted to them in release from illness and suffering. Thus, with the disciples, they followed the Saviour, testifying of mercy and love, ministering to his needs as opportunity presented itself. Service in the kingdom and to the Saviour and his circle of disciples became their holy privilege. From the first days of successful ministry, through the last months of growing hostility, to the very crest of Calvary, these women remained loyal.[4] Luke summarizes it thus:

> And the women, who had come with him out of Galilee, followed after, and beheld the tomb, and how his body was laid. And they returned, and prepared spices and ointments.[5]

The lodging-place to which they returned may well have

[1]Matt. 20:55 (Mark 16:1; Luke 23:49).   [2]Luke 24:10.   [3]Luke. 8:2.   [4]Luke 23:49.   [5]Luke 23:55, 56.

been the home of Mary of Jerusalem, even though Luke does not make a definite reference to her.[1]

Early on Easter morning, the first day of the week, these same women returned to the tomb, carrying the spices they had prepared for the embalming that had been interrupted by the coming of the Sabbath on Friday evening. These were the first of the Saviour's friends to venture to the sepulcher, save possibly the eager youth John Mark, son of Mary of Jerusalem. None of the disciples had even started before these women returned to the city telling of the Resurrection. Still so shocked by the Crucifixion were the men that

> . . . . these words appeared in their sight as idle talk; and they disbelieved them.[2]

This group, strengthened without doubt by Mary of Jerusalem and Mary and Martha of Bethany and the Saviour's own mother, formed the nucleus of devout women in the Church at Pentecost. They were instant in prayer, strong in faith, endowed with an alert spiritual intuition, active always in service. The love and devotion they bore to the Saviour was carried over in increasing effectiveness into the life and work of the growing Church.

Mary of Magdala

Chief among these women of Galilee was Mary Magdalene. Wherever they are mentioned by name, hers appears first. She was of the town of Magdala,[3] one of the fishing communities strung along the western shore of the Sea of Galilee from Capernaum southward past Roman Tiberias. Luke, the physician, speaks of her as

> . . . . Mary that was called Magdalene, from whom seven demons had gone out.[4]

---

[1]Review the section on the Early Church in this lovely home.
[2]Luke 24:11 (Mark 16:11).

[3]Today there is a squalid village on the site called Mejdel.
[4]Luke 8:2.

Of the evangelists it would be Luke whose use of medical terms could be counted on for precise meaning. The theory of demon-possession was commonly accepted as the explanation of what we today call epilepsy, and of various types of abnormal mental states. Numerous instances are recorded in the New Testament,[1] and nowhere is the term demon-possession used except in cases of this sort. It was a medical term, applicable to the varied forms of nervous and mental disorder. It was never employed with reference to sin or immorality, having no proper usage in the realm of moral habit. What Luke meant, in this reference to Mary of Magdala, was that she had suffered from a very severe type of chronic nervous or mental malady, and that she had been completely cured by the Saviour. In his statement there is not the least justification for thinking of her as having ever lived as a person of notorious immorality.

In the literature of the Early Church, both in the Scriptures themselves and in the writings of the first three centuries, Mary of Magdala is mentioned always with high respect as a woman of exemplary character and grace. Not until the fourth century are comments found that would identify her with the anonymous sinner described by Luke as washing the Saviour's feet with penitential tears while he reclined at dinner with Simon the Pharisee.[2] No satisfactory identification of this person had been made, and it occurred to some student in the fourth century that she might have been Mary of Magdala. The fact that her name appeared in the next chapter with the use of the phrase "seven demons" seemed to add color to the theory. It did not occur to the scribe that the casting out of demons had nothing to do

[1]Matt. 9:32-34; 17:14-21. Mark 1:32-34. Luke 4:31 ff.; 8:26 ff. Acts 16:16-18.
[2]Luke 7:36-50.

with questions of moral conduct, but was a technical medical term for mental disorders.

The utterly fallacious theory grew until it found complete acceptance throughout the Mediaeval Church. The Magdalene thus became the penitent from moral leprosy, rather than the agonized mental sufferer restored to blessed sanity. Indeed, the very name Magdalene has become in polite English a word to connote "reformed prostitute." Thus, for fifteen hundred years the youthful character of one of the saintliest of women has been tarnished in the thinking of multitudes, through error. Competent scholars can hardly find words strong enough to express their feeling. H. V. Morton speaks of the malevolent power of such a legend.[1] Findley calls it "libel."[2] The eminent English Bible student Geikie writes, "Never perhaps has a figment so utterly baseless obtained so wide acceptance."

In solemn phrase the writer of the Fourth Gospel records that with the beloved disciple, John,

> . . . . There were standing by the cross of Jesus his mother, and his mother's sister, Mary the wife of Clopas, and Mary Magdalene.[3]

All others had fled, or stood so far off that they were unrecognized in the gathering gloom. These alone remained steadfast in the hours of indescribable agony. Tender solicitude for his mother prompted the Saviour to commend her to John as his mother,

> . . . . And from that hour the disciple took her unto his own home.[4]

Seeing Christ alone in resurrection glory, James, his brother, came to serve the Church as its first stalwart leader; but John the faithful held the honor of caring for Mary as though he were actually her son. To the Emmaus

---

[1] See his *Women of the Bible* (New York: Dodd, Mead & Company, 1946), pp. 194, 195.
[2] J. A. Findley, ABC, article "Luke," p. 1039.
[3] John 19:25.
[4] John 19:27.

home of Mary, wife of Clopas, came the wondrous revelation of the Saviour when her husband and his friend took the Christ home with them in the dusk of Easter evening, unrecognized until he broke the bread.

Yet, to Mary Magdalene was granted the ineffable privilege of being the first to whom the risen Saviour showed himself at Easter's dawn. She, with the other Galilean women, had gone to the sepulcher at the light of day. Finding the stone rolled away

> She runneth therefore, and cometh to Simon Peter, and to the other disciple whom Jesus loved, and saith unto them, They have taken away the Lord out of the tomb, and we know not where they have laid him.[1]

Peter and John forthwith rushed to the sepulcher, and then returned to the city again, groping for faith,

> For as yet they knew not the scripture, that he must rise again from the dead.[2]

Mary Magdalene went again alone to the garden, standing in tears beside the open entrance of the tomb, striving to find her way through a maze of conflicting emotion. To her, then, came the Lord, sealing her loyalty and faith in this first revelation of himself to any of his followers. Words then spoken to her constitute one of his great commissions to believers everywhere:

> . . . . go unto my brethren, and say to them, I ascend unto my Father and your Father, and my God and your God.[3]

"THE ADVANCE" OF THE MODERN CHURCH

Soon the disciples journeyed "unto the mountain where Jesus had appointed them."[4] There they received the other

---

[1]John 20:2.   [3]John 20:17.
[2]John 20:9.   [4]Matt. 28:16.

solemn commission for the Church of all time, with the assurance of his continuing presence:

> . . . . All authority hath been given unto me in heaven and on earth. Go ye therefore, and make disciples of all the nations, baptizing them into the name of the Father and of the Son and of the Holy Spirit: teaching them to observe all things whatsoever I commanded you: and lo, I am with you always, even unto the end of the world.[1]

The history of nineteen centuries lies between the utterance of these words and the duty of the Church through which we serve the living Lord. However strange to patriarch or apostle might seem our way of life, incomprehensible at many points, vital prayer, daring faith, compelling love, and devoted service would still hold the ageless meanings they had known. They would be readily at home wherever these spiritual powers abide.

These ancients would note with amazed joy the place of women in the total Church. Sarah could walk the long and lonely journeys with missionary women carrying the Word of life to alien peoples. Rahab would understand her undaunted sisters as they planned for nobler living amidst the rubble of their cities. Naomi and Ruth and the woman of Sychar would sense the deep undertones of unity women speak today in areas where race tensions prevail. Lydia would love the far-flung marts we know and the women who guide in the business of the world. Lois and Eunice would pray for every home from which youth bravely ventures to the ends of the earth. Hannah would enter every church school she could visit, and Mary of Jerusalem with Mary of Magdala would bless the plans of every group of Christian women they could find. Priscilla would grasp the problems of those who seek to train the brilliant young leaders of tomorrow.

[1]Matt. 28:18-20.

The marvel they would see is the mighty organization of the women of the Church. At home, abroad, in every strata of need, our women serve. They build a shrine for prayer, and keep the candles ever lit. They strengthen faith by every faculty of mind and heart. They serve in worship, song, and praise. They toil for nobler homelife, and justice as found in the Word. These women of the past would rejoice in the broad scope of women's service in the Church today.

OUR TASK

The world stands before its most tremendous crisis of choice. Two concepts of human worth, of life, of goodness, of God himself, are at grips. This has often occurred in the centuries gone. But now the field of struggle includes the total of human life; the issues are vaster, more profound than those faced by earlier generations.

Delinquency and disrespect for law are rampant. Sin is insidious, and unrighteousness walks in public places. Secularism, which laughs at prayer and devotion, corrodes the faith without which men cannot truly live. A social and political philosophy that declares a person to be but a gadget of the state, knowing no morality save the expediency of the moment, blatantly challenges Christ's teaching of the worth of man, and divine meaning of the Cross. The Church of Christ is embattled in every sector of human life, along the whole of its great perimeter. It is a struggle in which no quarter can be asked or expected of the adversary.

But in such a day defense is not enough. Merely to hold the line will never win the world. To advance in every sector, to attack without cessation, seizing the initiative and maintaining it, is the Church's only answer. This involves the full development and maintenance of every spiritual resource that prayer, faith, and consecration can offer. The careful planning of strategy is required across the world, and through all the social order. For ourselves, as Methodists, we call it "The Advance for Christ and His Church." The Woman's Society of Christian Service, including the Wesleyan Service Guild, while working diligently for the advance of the entire church, has its own "Four-Point Program of Advance." Communions other than The Methodist Church are equally alert, and together we all pray, plan, and serve.

Bringing to a conclusion his careful study, "Secularism and the Christian Faith," Bishop G. Bromley Oxnam said:[1]

> A secularized society can be transformed into a spiritual society when individuals live the life of the spirit wherever they may serve. This is to lay hold upon spiritual forces that are more powerful than political or economic forces. This is to recognize that when the Kingdom of God is within us and living within us and expressed by us, society itself can become the Kingdom.

Yet, faint hearts may quail. Small spirits shrivel in the heat of struggle. And many fear the seeming equal balance of contending forces, and dread uncertainty stifles hope and unnerves the arm. In a recent radio sermon Bishop Oxnam forthrightly declared:

> There are blessings in uncertainty: the joy of walking in the untraveled Way, the exhilaration of laying hold on unfolding Truth, the satisfaction of sharing in the unending Life. There is yet more meaning in Christ's word, "I am the Way, the Truth, and the Life".[2]

These richer meanings shall appear as, stone by stone, the Way is built on which all men may walk erect and unafraid; as, word by word, the Truth of God lives in mankind's thought and speech; as, pulse by pulse, pure and clear, the glad free life of God fills all the world.

---

[1] In one of a series of talks made by various speakers at Evanston Conference in 1947, later edited by J. Richard Spann, under the title, *The Christian Faith and Secularism* (New York and Nashville: Abingdon-Cokesbury Press, 1947), p. 288.

[2] G. Bromley Oxnam, *The Stimulus of Christ* (New York: Fleming H. Revell Co., 1947), p. 37.

SUGGESTIONS FOR FURTHER STUDY

1. Read the accounts concerning Dorcas (Acts 9:36-43) and Ananias and Sapphira (Acts 5:1-11). Contrast the types of service they rendered to the Church. Evaluate the immortality of reputation associated with their names.

2. Note carefully all the references you can find regarding the women disciples from Galilee. Use a good concordance, and read every suggested marginal reference in your Bible. List the personal characteristics of these women. Place in parallel columns the various types of service the biblical women rendered and those offered in the Woman's Society of Christian Service today.

3. Select for special attention a major character discussed in a preceding chapter. Re-read the section concerning her. Study the biblical references, from the point of view of faith. Show how memory, reason, affection, conscience, will, formed part of her faith. As a group project, let several characters be chosen for a study of contrasting elements in their faith.

4. Note the instances of prayer that occur in one of the Gospels. Describe the types of service-experience directly connected with the prayer, telling the kind of faith exemplified in the incident. Indicate how prayer, faith, and service were all a part of the experience.

Index of References
For Women of Scripture

Woman's Division of Christian Service
Board of Missions and Church Extension
The Methodist Church
Literature Headquarters: 420 Plum Street, Cincinnati 2, Ohio
Price, 60 cents